MW01289885

from Doug Perry

Fellowship Of The Martyrs

Copyright © 2011 Doug Perry, Fellowship Of The Martyrs

fotm@fellowshipofthemartyrs.com
www.FellowshipOfTheMartyrs.com

All rights reserved.

ISBN: 1467963879
ISBN-13: 978-1467963879

Cover artwork (Dad in chair) by Fred Arndt
Logos and graphic editing by Doug Perry
All Copyright © 2011, Fellowship Of The Martyrs

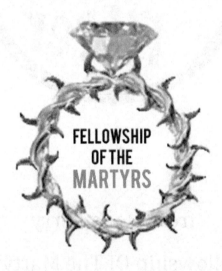

The Bride gets her jewelry, but it's going to hurt to get it on, and
once you're used to it, you're never going to want to rip it back
off again. Heaven is free. HOLINESS is hard!
If not us, who? If not here, where? If not now, when?

DEDICATION

First this book is dedicated to Father God. He told me in 2006 that if I would not look back, He would care for me as a father cares for a son, and He has been absolutely true to that ever since. I'm sorry it took me so long to submit and obey and rely fully on You, Dad. Please forgive me and help me to do better. I love You, Dad.

And this book is dedicated to my Earth Dad, Bob Perry. He is truly as good a man as I imagine that any man can be. I have counseled with people whose dad locked them in the trunk of a car with dead cats, who hired them out as a prostitute at eight years old, who was never there, who beat them mercilessly. One of the foundational memories in my life was that I knew that, though Dad was busy, he always told his secretary that if his boys called, it didn't matter how important the meeting, we were to be put right through. I always knew that if someday I was arrested walking down Main Street, cross-dressing, drunk, high, soliciting sex from a police officer – I could still come home and he'd love me. He came to my sporting events, to my recitals, spoke at my graduation and more. He would pull me onto his lap and kiss my boo-boos and tell me how much he loved me and that I could do anything. He sacrificed a lot. I know how blessed I am – and how truly rare my experience is.

Every woman in my life that was ever important to me was molested or raped or abused. Some by their fathers. So many people that I deal with have absolutely NO concept of what a polite relationship with a dad might be like, much less loving. There are so many times when the good "Dad stuff" in me HAD to be there in order to minister to them.

So, I thank you again, Dad. I've said it before, but I really don't think I could do my job without you having done your job really, really well. I love you, Dad. (And Mom, too.)

CONTENTS

ACKNOWLEDGMENTS

This book really should not be read all on its own. It is a part of a larger understanding, a series of books written about what is wrong with "church." The statistics are covered in the book, "*The Apology To The World.*" The book, "*The Red Dragon: the horrifying truth about why the 'church' cannot seem to change*" extends on this and shows the supernatural roots and the solution to wipe the slate clean and reboot. The book, "*Do It Yourself City Church Restoration*" lays the foundation scripturally for what Church should look like and how we rebuild this. And the book, "*DEMONS?! You're kidding right?*" shows how it's under attack and how to defend it. Before we can fix a system, we have to fix each individual, so for personal tune-ups, the book, "*Dialogues with God*" is helpful to learn to hear God better and "*Who Neutered The Holy Spirit?!*" is for those who think God isn't as supernatural as He used to be.

God has been pouring out a lot on Liberty, Missouri. We continue to pray and believe that this will be a refuge, a haven, a training and equipping center.

If you're looking for a different kind of "church," something more real and more life-changing, and if the Lord leads, you're welcome in Liberty. When (not if) things hit the fan, if you can make it here, we'll do our best to love you and make a way together through all that is coming.

www.FellowshipOfTheMartyrs.com
fotm@fellowshipofthemartyrs.com

WHO AM I?

Well, I'm not entirely pleased with the idea of starting a book this way, but if you're going to understand what this is all about, it seems reasonable to know where I'm coming from. My name is Doug Perry. I grew up the son of a preacher and missionaries. I went to college planning on going into full-time ministry as a pastor – I mean, my dad was one and I'm twice as smart as him, so how hard could it really be? I soon got disenchanted with the politics of the Southern Baptist Convention and sought to broaden my horizons. I graduated in 1989 from William Jewell College in Liberty, Missouri with Bachelors degrees in Religion and Psychology. Frustrated with the "church" system, I went into the business world, starting in human resources and ending up as Vice President of Marketing for a young restaurant delivery company in Herndon, Virginia that was just starting to franchise all over the country.

It took about a year and a half for me to really hate the Washington D.C. area. I longed to be back at William Jewell working with students. I wrote an impassioned letter to the President of the college and he encouraged me to contact the Dean of Students. The Dean encouraged me to get a Masters degree. So I got accepted at the University of Missouri – Kansas City and began work on a degree in Education – particularly Higher Education Administration.

Various self-employed business adventures ensued, some distracting from course work, but I eventually finished in the Spring of 1994 and took a job as Director of Residence Life and Student Life at St. Mary College in Leavenworth, Kansas. As in any small college, one is often tapped to multi-task, so at times I was Risk-Management officer, Counselor, Student Activities Director, Cheerleading Coach and the Men's Tennis Coach. And I sat on three Inauguration Committees for three Presidents – all in three years.

During this time I applied all the Psychology I'd learned in college and all the Counseling, Group Process and other skills learned at the university. And I must say, the results were better than the average practitioner applying psychology to a situation – that is to say, terrible. The campus was plagued with a reputation as the place to send "problem children" because "the nuns will take care of them." They were the preferred recommendation of any high school guidance counselor in the area to parents who didn't think their poor maladjusted child could handle a big state school. I could count on several suicide attempts or gestures every semester – along with drugs, alcohol, cutters, pregnancies and more. Not to mention the usual roommate conflicts, homesickness, boyfriend/girlfriend stresses, sudden death in the family and other standard college things.

Overall, I handled it very well – in the context of what I knew then. I did sincerely love the resident students and knew them all by name. I spent a lot of time with them, far beyond the requirements of the job. But I wish I knew then what I know now. I think the outcomes would have been dramatically different – certainly for their souls. However, it's HIGHLY doubtful that the Catholic administration would have allowed me the freedom to really get them free.

After three years at the college, I left and started my own business doing antique furniture restoration. Within a couple of years I had an unlisted phone number and a six month backlog of work. In 2001, I put some of the products we were selling on the side (solid wood furniture, antique hardware, custom table pads) on a website and our "dot com" era started. It grew 20% month over month for five years. We could manage it from home for the first year, but then had to move into a showroom, then a bigger showroom. At the peak we had thirteen employees (several who were stay-at-home moms), we were doing about $220,000 a month in sales, with over 250,000 products on our websites. We were twice named the most "family-friendly" workplace in Kansas City and in 2005 we were the number four fastest growing company in the Metro area and named one of the top 25 businesses under 25 employees.

I don't say any of this to brag. God had me throw all the trophies and awards and newspaper articles in the dumpster. In 2004 when God got ahold of me and shook me to my core,

I threw out pretty much everything I had ever learned from church or school or business – and let Him reboot me. I began to learn how God sees the things that we normally use psychological terms to describe. I began to see that the Gifts of Spirit are real and that they work. I was particularly shocked by the gift of Discernment of Spirits when the Lord dialed mine up really high and I started seeing demons. Then we started a food pantry out of the back of the furniture store, missionaries started being sent by God to volunteer at my for-profit business. People were getting healed and delivered of demons in the showroom! Then in 2006 God said walk away and don't look back – and I watched them throw everything in a dumpster.

Now, with God's help, I manage a food pantry feeding 5,000 people per month, group homes housing 50-70+ people, I've written seven books, made hundreds of videos and audios, seen millions of hits on our websites, counseled with hard-cases like you could barely imagine, dealt with things FAR worse than at the college (including people setting themselves on fire, race wars and knife fights!) and I'm pretty well dependent on God for everything all the time. I've seen demons do some really wild things through people. I regularly get calls from people wanting to know how to keep unseen things from throwing them around the house or raping them in their sleep.

OK, now this is where I typically lose people, but I'm asking you to just hang with me and hear me out. If it helps you to cope with all this demon talk, just imagine that I'm speaking metaphorically or poetically, that's fine. I don't mind you watering it down so your head doesn't explode, but

I think you ought to hear me out on this. There are days that even the tiny little shred of Southern Baptist that is left in ME kind of thinks I'm crazy – but then I see the results.

I can stand as a witness on both sides and say that I've handled really difficult counseling situations using all the Psychology learned from two institutions of higher education – and I've also handled them the way Jesus did. And I can state unequivocally that Jesus' methods just plain work WAY better. So much so that I've gladly deleted from my internal hard drive nearly all the things I learned in the schools of Man.

Stay with me here and I think you'll see what I mean. I used to hop from career to career every couple of years because I was bored, but since November 23, 2004 I've been on the most amazing roller coaster ride imaginable. It's cost me everything to get here, but I wouldn't trade it for anything! I love my job and I hope you will see why.

HOW DID I FIND IT?

Well, I don't really keep a journal so it's hard for me to pinpoint a date, but it was in December of 2004 when I began to see demons on people. The more I practiced and was a good steward with what He gave me, the more refined it got. In Matthew 25, Jesus says that if He gives you something – whether a little or a lot – and you're a good steward, He will multiply it abundantly. But if you bury it in the sand and are selfish, even that will be taken from you. So I invested it wisely, I used it to help people, to get them free – and I got more.

This is not the place for a talk on all the different kinds of demons, what they look like, where they hide and how to get them off. That's all in my book "DEMONS?! You're kidding, right?" But for the purposes of this book, let me say that I began to see in the spirit. For people that don't know what that means, it's like a knowing that something is there, but you can't see it with "natural" eyes. It was kind of like seeing what was behind the veil that separates this world from reality. (Most people think THIS world is reality, but having seen both, I can assure you that this is like a foggy, black and white dream compared to the other side.) At the most basic level, you just know something is wrong with that person and you don't want to be around them. Maybe you have a "sense" of a black cloud around them. But if you get dialed up far enough, you'll see snakes and frogs and generational curses and soul ties and you'll know they got molested by sweaty Uncle Ed when they were five and they have unforgiveness toward their mother – and whatever else the Lord is willing to show you.

I remember a person came in the Spring of 2005 and I was just looking them over and praying to see what the Lord would show me was a problem for them and I saw a strange black, hockey puck-shaped thing in their right hip. I'd never seen it before and had no idea what it was. It wasn't the kind of thing where I figured it out over time or had a very large sample size to compare lots of people and find commonalities. I saw it for the first time, asked the Lord what it was, and He told me it was a "Dad Filter."

Doesn't that just seem so much easier than sample groups and statistical analyses and personality inventories and years of interviews on couches? I sure like it better!

(Oh, and if you don't hear God but want to, we have resources to help with that in the book, "Dialogues with God." If you don't think God speaks to people anymore, I would suggest our book, "Who Neutered the Holy Spirit?!")

WHAT IS IT?

When I saw this strange black "hockey puck" in their hip, I asked the Lord what it was. He said, "It's a Dad Filter. It's a lens they look at Me through that is shaped like Earth Dad. It's a box they have put me in." Then I would really press in and ask more questions about how long it had been there, what it looked like, and whatever else I could think of. Sometimes God would give me VERY specific information, sometimes just a sense of the problem.

The Bible says that God gives us the keys to the Kingdom, that as joint heirs with Jesus we have access to all things, that we will do greater things than He did – and it says that if we bind it on earth it will be bound in heaven and if we loose it on earth it will be loosed in heaven.

Matthew 16:19 – And I will give unto thee the keys of the kingdom of heaven: and whatsoever thou shalt bind on earth shall be bound in heaven: and whatsoever thou shalt loose on earth shall be loosed in heaven.

John 14:12-13 – Verily, verily, I say unto you, he that believeth on me, the works that I do shall he do also; and greater [works] than these shall he do; because I go unto my Father. And whatsoever ye shall ask in my name, that will I do, that the Father may be glorified in the Son.

Now, some people will say that the promises of Matthew 16:19 were for Peter only (and the Popes), but all of us are joint heirs with Christ and adopted sons and have access to the Throne of God. (And that whole Pope thing is fiction.)

Romans 8:15-17 – For ye have not received the spirit of bondage again to fear; but ye have received the Spirit of adoption, whereby we cry, Abba, Father. The Spirit itself beareth witness with our spirit, that we are the children of God. And if children, then heirs; heirs of God and joint-heirs with Christ; if so be that we suffer with [him], that we may be also glorified together.

Galatians 4:6 – And because ye are sons, God has sent forth the Spirit of his Son into your hearts, crying, Abba, Father.

There are a couple of really important things in that passage we need to point out. First is that this is a verse of which VERY few people grasp the fullness of the imperative sense of "Abba." It is Father, but more desperate. In the Chaldee language it became used in prayer so much that it sort of became a sacred name for God, but it is an emphatic tense, more like a child in pain would cry out, "DADDY!"

The other point is that as heirs with Christ, we have access to all that to which He has access. Peter was not the only apostle, or believer, or adopted son. I know the reality of binding and loosing. Our words have power and we all need to be a LOT more careful with our words.

But then He also says that we can limit Him and get in His way by our lack of faith!

Matthew 21:21 – Jesus answered and said unto them, Verily I say unto you, If ye have faith, and doubt not, ye shall not only do this [which is done] to the fig tree, but also if ye shall say unto this mountain, Be thou removed, and be thou cast into the sea; it shall be done.

Matthew 17:20 – And Jesus said unto them, Because of your unbelief: for verily I say unto you, If ye have faith as a grain of mustard seed, ye shall say unto this mountain, Remove hence to yonder place; and it shall remove; and nothing shall be impossible unto you.

If you have even the tiniest bit of faith, like a mustard seed, the smallest of all seeds, then you can move mountains. If you have the tiniest little sliver of Jesus in you, it's more than enough authority to do any miracle. But just a TINY bit of YOU can keep it from happening! That's an example of how our own faith, our own beliefs and expectations, can bind things up.

Matthew 9:27-30 – And when Jesus departed thence, two blind men followed him, crying, and saying, [Thou] Son of David, have mercy on us. And when he was come into the house, the blind men came to him: and Jesus saith unto them, Believe ye that I am able to do this? They said unto him, Yea, Lord. Then touched he their eyes, saying, According to your faith be it unto you. And their eyes were opened and Jesus straitly charged them, saying, See [that] no man know [it].

So one of the very first things we have to do here to help people get unclogged and walk in the fullness of what He has for them is to deal this "Dad Filter."

It's kind of like a lens, like a filter that you look at God through that puts limits on Him. Like putting God in a box. Like blinders on a racehorse so that all it can see is what's straight ahead. A lot of times people don't realize they've done it. It's something they learned very early in life from Earth Dad. It's like a cookie-cutter shaped like Earth Dad that you try to squeeze God into.

I counseled with one sister whose dad threw her in the trunk of a car with dead cats – and another whose father would lock her in the closet and invite people to come home from the bar and molest her for money. When you go through those kinds of things and then pray, "Our Father who aren't in heaven, hallowed be thy name," it's really mangled up. It's hard to have a right relationship with Father God when you've never had a dad at all, or he was a jerk – or worse.

There are all kinds of different Dad Filters – layers even – and God will help you unravel them. But I want you to spend some time thinking about how your relationship with Father God might be looking a lot like your relationship with Earth Dad.

I counseled with this brother in Texas one time. He had a huge, huge spirit of fear and anxiety. He was on all kinds of medications for depression and anxiety. He was barely surviving in Dallas, but God was calling him to India! And he didn't know how to handle even what he was going through right now. It was freaking him out. He was doing so much in his own power.

So I asked the Lord, "Can we pray and get the spirit of fear off of him?"

And the Lord says, "No, you can't."

I said, "Why not?"

"Because of the Dad Filter."

So I press in and ask the Lord more questions about what he's been through – and it's horrible, just horrible.

So I ask the Lord, "Can we deal with the Dad Filter?"

"Yeah, talk to him about that."

And I've done this a lot so I talk to him and I say, "Brother, you know all those times your dad would push you on the swings and kiss your boo-boos and pull you up on his lap and tell you how proud he was of you and you could do anything? You remember all those times?"

He said, "No. My dad died when I was two."

"Yeah. So … string of step-dads and Mom's boyfriends that would beat on you and you learned to keep your head down and hide and do everything in your own power – because mom wouldn't help and nobody would really come to your rescue?"

"Yeah, how did you know?"

"Well, that's just what the Lord's telling me. Can you understand that you learned that as a very small child that Dads WILL NOT come to your rescue, they're going to abandon you, they're untrustworthy and you pretty much have to do everything yourself? And you've got all this fear and stuff messing with you, but you're kind of rebuking it in the name of YOU because you don't think anyone else will come to help? And that's just never going to work – the demons messing with you are not the least bit afraid of you. They just chuckle when you try that. If it's not Jesus, it's just never going to work. But you don't think He'll come and help."

And he kind of started to see it. It's not so much demonic, you can't just rebuke it off – it's a lie. When a grain of sand gets into the shell of an oyster, it irritates it so it secretes a fluid and makes a pearl. The longer it's there, the bigger and bigger it gets. Like the oyster, we probably don't even realize we're doing it. That's why Dad's are important, because they shape our understanding of who Father God is. And they're supposed to help us transition while we're small from the natural dad to the spiritual dad. But if they're not there or they're mangled, we can't transition smoothly to Father God. And we end up with a distorted or partial perception of who Father God really is.

My job is to hold up a mirror and show people, "Do you see that you're doing this? Do you see that you put God in a box shaped like THAT guy? That even though you preach that God is love and he'll come to your rescue and you quote Psalm 23 and all of that – that you don't believe it. Because of your experience with Earth Dad, you don't think God will be there for you like that."

And he kind of started to see it, so we prayed and I said, "What we need to do is repent because you're telling God that you're SO special that He can love everybody but you – and that's just arrogance and pride. Like your badness can outweigh His goodness. You don't get to dictate the terms of the relationship with God. He's big and you're little and you don't get to do that. You don't get a say."

It's like if you have a thirteen year old daughter, and she's going through her Goth-wearing, cranky, parents-are-stupid phase. And she comes down from her room every morning and grouses at you and only talks to you when she wants money and won't invite her friends over because she's embarrassed of you and thinks you are stupid and ugly. But you'll take whatever you can get because you're her dad, you're her mom, and you'll take what you can get and you love her. But you'll pray and hope she gets over it and endure through it and try to make the most of it. But it would be SO much better if she came down every morning and kissed your forehead and wanted to go to the mall with you and was your best friend and wanted to talk to you about the boy she just met. That would be so much better, but you'll take whatever you can get.

She's a kid – she shouldn't get to dictate the terms of the relationship. But you love her and you'll let her and you'll just pray she'll get over it. That's what Father God has been doing with you – and so many other people. If we only come to Him when someone is in the hospital or we need a job or someone is in jail, and we just think He's like a fire extinguisher – He'll take it. But it would be so much better if you were just holding His hand all the time, if you really believed that He will push you on the swing-set and kiss your boo-boos and pat your head and stuff.

You may have never had a dad like that and may not even be able to get your head around how God could do that – but I can assure that God does, that He says He will and He does. My best prayer for you would be that you would take that lens, that filter – the blinders that are leaving out all the parts of God that don't conveniently fitting into your experience, your world-view, your sense of what you think Dad's are – and just say you're sorry. Because it's pride, it's arrogance in the extreme, it's the same as the lie of the snake in the Garden to say, "Well, God didn't really mean that. He's not really like that. He may be like that with other people but not with me." It's a lie.

And I just want you to say you're sorry. Go to Him and say, "I'm sorry that I put you in a box. I'm sorry that I limited you in any way. I'm sorry that I dictated the terms of this relationship. Please just take that lens and bash it up into a million pieces and don't let me put you in a box anymore. You just swoop in and be God to me in whatever way you want. I want to hold your hand, I want to talk to you. I want to walk with you all the time. Show me what kind of a Dad you are."

So I prayed that with that brother in Dallas. And we took the Sword of the Spirit and bashed that little hockey puck up into a million pieces. And while he was praying (and crying), the Father told me, "As soon as he bashes up that lens, I want you to pounce on him like Tiger and hug the stuffing out of him and tell him how much I love him and rip off the spirit of fear and the loneliness and help him get his cup full." So I did. He wasn't used to hugging at all – but I outweighed him by about a hundred pounds so he didn't have much choice. It turned out that he was really desperate for a hug, and he was pretty good at it. And we both cried and he got free. What an honor to be the hands and feet (and hugs) of God!

We're going to move on from here to give a lot more detail on all the permutations of this. Don't stop now just because you think you got the general idea. It's a lot more subtle than that. There are some great case studies in the pages to come and some things that I think you really need to hear. Not just to be useful to help other people get free – but for your own walk with the Lord.

Keep reading!

SUPERNATURAL VS PSYCHOLOGICAL

We always have a choice whether to see things through carnal eyes or spiritual eyes. To describe things the way the world does or the way God does. To handle problems led by the Spirit or led by "common sense." I find that "common sense" is usually not very common and doesn't particularly make sense in the light of eternity.

Romans 8:6 – For to be carnally minded [is] death; but to be spiritually minded [is] life and peace.

I Corinthians 13:11 – When I was a child, I spake as a child, I understood as a child, I thought as a child: but when I became a man, I put away childish things.

If you call yourself a "Christian" then you ought to be a follower of Christ – and that means seeing things His way and not the way of the World. Man should not define terms for you, but rather God. Few things chap my hide more than pastors using all the tools of psychology instead of faith. In the Bible we see Jesus dealing with a variety of strange behaviors that today we would diagnose medically.

Matthew 17:14-21 – And when they were come to the multitude, there came to him a certain man, kneeling down to him, and saying, Lord, have mercy on my son: for he is lunatick, and sore vexed: for ofttimes he falleth into the fire, and oft into the water. And I brought him to thy disciples, and they could not cure him.

Then Jesus answered and said, O faithless and perverse generation, how long shall I be with you? how long shall I suffer you? bring him hither to me. And Jesus rebuked the devil; and he departed out of him: and the child was cured from that very hour. Then came the disciples to Jesus apart, and said, Why could not we cast him out? And Jesus said unto them, Because of your unbelief: for verily I say unto you, If ye have faith as a grain of mustard seed, ye shall say unto this mountain, Remove hence to yonder place; and it shall remove; and nothing shall be impossible unto you. Howbeit this kind goeth not out but by prayer and fasting.

That word "lunatick" was most often used in reference to someone that we would call epileptic. In fact, in some of the newer Bible translations (RSV, for example), it just says right there that the child is epileptic. The response of Jesus is not to medicate him or institutionalize him, but deliver him of a demon. And it's clear that other people (the disciples) had tried without success. So Jesus lectures to them about their own faith (filters) and the need for a lifestyle of prayer and fasting in order to deal with certain kinds of demons.

There are lots more examples. Here in Luke 8 we see a woman with a blood problem (probably hemophilia) who had tried all the "scientific" methods, been to all the doctors, and all they did was take her money and leave her worse off. (The story is repeated in Mark 5.) But she heard the stories about Jesus, had faith and believed that THERE was the solution to her problems. All she did was touch Him in the midst of a crowd and sucked out the healing she needed.

> Luke 8:43-48 – And a woman having an issue of blood twelve years, which had spent all her living upon physicians, neither could be healed of any, came behind him, and touched the border of his garment: and immediately her issue of blood stanched. And Jesus said, Who touched me? When all denied, Peter and they that were with him said, Master, the multitude throng thee and press thee, and sayest thou, Who touched me? And Jesus said, Somebody hath touched me: for I perceive that virtue is gone out of me. And when the woman saw that she was not hid, she came trembling, and falling down before him, she declared unto him before all the people for what cause she had touched him, and how she was healed immediately. And he said unto her, Daughter, be of good comfort: thy faith hath made thee whole; go in peace.

That word "virtue" is sometimes translated "power." It is the Greek word "dunamis" or "dynamis" (depending on the lexicon) and is the word from which we derive "dynamite." It is no small thing and Jesus was so aware of the state of this power within Him that He could tell that some drained out. We talk more about that in the book, "Rain Right <u>NOW</u>,

Lord!" The reality is that the Bible shows that this power of God is transferrable and all of us should be learning how to do stay full of that power.

Here's another example. What kind of medical diagnosis would you give this guy?

Mark 5:1-20 – And they came over unto the other side of the sea, into the country of the Gadarenes. And when he was come out of the ship, immediately there met him out of the tombs a man with an unclean spirit, who had his dwelling among the tombs; and no man could bind him, no, not with chains: because that he had been often bound with fetters and chains, and the chains had been plucked asunder by him, and the fetters broken in pieces: neither could any man tame him. And always, night and day, he was in the mountains, and in the tombs, crying, and cutting himself with stones. But when he saw Jesus afar off, he ran and worshipped him, and cried with a loud voice, and said, What have I to do with thee, Jesus, thou Son of the most high God? I adjure thee by God, that thou torment me not.

For he said unto him, Come out of the man, thou unclean spirit. And he asked him, What is thy name? And he answered, saying, My name is Legion: for we are many. And he besought him much that he would not send them away out of the country. Now there was there nigh unto the mountains a great herd of swine feeding. And all the devils besought him, saying, Send us into the swine, that we may enter into them. And forthwith Jesus gave them leave. And the unclean spirits went out, and entered into the swine: and the herd ran violently down a steep place into the sea, (they were about two thousand;) and were choked in the sea.

And they that fed the swine fled, and told it in the city, and in the country. And they went out to see what it was that was done. And they come to Jesus, and see him that was possessed with the devil, and had the legion, sitting, and clothed, and in his right mind: and they were afraid. And they that saw it told them how it befell to him that was possessed with the devil, and also concerning the swine. And they began to pray him to depart out of their coasts.

And when he was come into the ship, he that had been possessed with the devil prayed him that he might be with him. Howbeit Jesus suffered him not, but saith unto him, Go home to thy friends, and tell them how great things the Lord hath done for thee, and hath had compassion on thee. And he departed, and began to publish in Decapolis how great things Jesus had done for him: and all men did marvel.

Wow. That story is jam packed with crazy! OK, you have a guy that is living in the tombs, so strong that nobody can restrain him, exhibiting schizophrenia, depression, cutting, multiple personalities, and more. This is a PRIME candidate for psychotropic drugs! Can you imagine how a person like this would be handled in the United States today? There would be police called in (maybe SWAT) and they'd taze him and drug the life out of him and lock him down somewhere.

The Bible makes absolutely ZERO effort to describe this as a medical condition. It's clearly presented as demons – and a lot of demons at that – unlike in other scenarios, Jesus doesn't just cast out the demons, he lets them go into the pigs (an unclean animal) and the pigs freak out and commit suicide. The townspeople are terrified by the miracle, seeing this man they all know sitting there in his right mind, and they're fairly irritated at losing a couple of thousand pigs.

They beg Jesus to leave the area and He complies. Now, if you were that guy that was living in the tombs and cutting himself, you can pretty well figure that you are VERY grateful and you don't really have anywhere else to go after years of alienating everyone you loved – so it's perfectly natural for him to be loyal to the guy that healed him. He wants to go with Jesus, but Jesus tells him to go instead and tell everyone what God has done for him.

In one of my videos I ask this trivia question – "Who was the first missionary Jesus ever sent out?" We see where Jesus sent out 70 of His disciples ahead of him in pairs (Matt. 18, Luke 10) and then sent the 12 out in pairs after that. You could say that the Samaritan woman at the well in John 4 went and told the story, but Jesus didn't send her. No, the first missionary Jesus ever sent out was THIS guy, the most demonized guy in the whole Bible. And unlike the disciples who were sent out in pairs, this guy goes alone, without healing or delivering demons – just telling his testimony, just telling about what Jesus did for him. And single-handedly he evangelizes the Decapolis – a region of ten cities! This is a real testament to the glory and grace of God to use the most foolish things to confound the wise.

1 Corinthians 1:27 – But God hath chosen the foolish things of the world to confound the wise; and God hath chosen the weak things of the world to confound the things which are mighty;

I can testify to the reality of this kind of healing. I went into the home of a young man who was suffering from agoraphobia with panic attacks (fear of public and open places). It took a lot of talking for his roommate to convince him to even let us in the house. He had gotten so bad that he would leave an envelope with money on the door, call to have a pizza delivered, they would leave it on the doorstep, take the money and once he saw them drive off he would snatch it off the porch and slam the door. He was unable to drive or work and was in very bad shape.

Rather than deal with it psychologically, we trusted that Jesus knew what He was doing and dealt with it Biblically. I asked the Lord what was going on. We identified some areas of unforgiveness in his heart, addressed his Dad Filter (Dad was never around, I'm on my own), he repented and then the Lord let me rebuke the spirit of fear that looked like a big black snake coiled around his head. Also confusion, loneliness, and double-mindedness – as I recall.

His roommate called me the very next day and said that he was out of the house trying to get his old job back and feeling great. I dare any psychiatrist to see that kind of instant result after spending about forty-five minutes with someone. Can you imagine how much less money they would make?! What a discretionary income destroyer it would be if people actually got healed in one session!

I've seen people instantly free from addictions to alcohol, prescription painkillers, cigarettes and more. One of the most remarkable was a brother instantly delivered from methadone with no side effects. To get off of methadone, you're basically talking about 30-45 days in bed, under medical care, weaning you off slowly, feeling like you were hit by a car and have the worst flu of your life at the same time. A brother came wanting to be free and we really felt like he should kick it here with us. He was fully expecting a horrible, painful experience but knew he had to get off of it. I wasn't hearing it would go like that. We obeyed the Bible.

James 5:14-15 – Is any sick among you? let him call for the elders of the church; and let them pray over him, anointing him with oil in the name of the Lord: And the prayer of faith shall save the sick, and the Lord shall raise him up; and if he have committed sins, they shall be forgiven him.

We prayed for him and waited. He stopped Methadone cold turkey – which NO medical professional would advise you to ever do. People die. He had no withdrawals – and his diabetes went away and the black necrotic (dead) tissue on his legs from the diabetes turned pink within a few days.

Now, I'm not claiming that every single person that we've prayed for got healed. There are things that can block their deliverance – like that they like their sin and don't really want to stop. Or their Dad Filter or other things. But we have seen remarkable success. I've seen people healed of epilepsy, lupus, fibromyalgia, chronic migraines, sleep apnea, diabetes, heart problems, all kinds of fears and addictions, stress related physical problems, ulcers, irritable bowel, I've seen bones healed instantly. I even had the great honor and blessing of watching the Lord radically reboot and heal more than one child with what had been diagnosed as advanced autism. So dramatic a transformation that the next day the teacher at the special needs day care could not believe it was the same kid.

Another transformation was so dramatic that the director of the orphanage where this three year old girl had been for nearly two years could not believe her eyes when she saw her two weeks later holding hands, obeying, eating with a fork politely and acting like any other kid. At the orphanage, one worker had to be assigned just to her at all times because she would break things and constantly being causing trouble. After being with us for just a few days, the situation was radically different. That's because it wasn't a chemical imbalance or brain damage, it was demons. We dealt with it spiritually, got them off, got her cup full of Jesus and everything changed.

Now, you can choose to dismiss my testimony altogether, but I'm not some hillbilly playing with snakes. I've been trained and I'm fundamentally a skeptic. I'm not the type to roll around on the floor or even shout and dance around. I'm a life-long Missouri mule – SHOW ME – I want it proven or I'm not going. A Missouri mule is the most stubborn animal alive. If it sits down and doesn't want to move you can't hit it enough, bribe it enough, yell at it enough – all you can do is hook the tractor to it and drag it into the barn. Anyone will tell you, I don't go easily.

I understand about placebo effects. I understand about groupthink and mass psychosis. I understand about mob mentalities and even the healing power of religious fervor or "good vibes" or positive thinking. But you can't positive think a healing on an autistic kid or instantly mend a broken bone. I don't believe you can placebo a withdrawal from long-term use of methadone. I'm telling you that I've seen things that responded instantly to prayer that I don't think a psychiatrist or a psychologist could have got to budge at all. Moreover, I've seen things respond to prayer when the subject didn't even know I was praying for them! (And I've seen plenty of times meds, psychiatrists and psychologists made things a lot worse.)

I know this isn't about me. I'm just a tool. I get that. And I'm not unique – lots of people have seen God move instantly and convincingly outside of the realm of science and medicine. And there are surely counterfeits and quacks – no doubt about it. But the fact that there are counterfeit $100 bills does not mean that the real ones don't exist. If we were truly going to be investigative, truly be open-minded to the possibilities, truly use the "scientific method," then we would search out whatever works and test it.

That's what I've done. I've seen both sides personally and in real practice. And I've never found anything that works better to get people free than to do it the way the Bible says to do it. Address the lies and crush them, teach them to test the voices in their head and bring them into obedience with Christ, show them that they are conquerors not victims, repent for any generational curses, lay down any unforgiveness in their hearts, stand firmly against any person

28

or demon or influence of any kind that is out to harm them. Works great.

There are a bunch of new books about the voices people hear, the "inner critic" versus the "inner coach." The inner critic is that thing that always whispers in your head and tells you to do bad things, tells you you're not good enough, that nothing you do will succeed, that you're a failure, that God could never love you. And the inner coach is that voice that encourages you, that reminds you of past victories, that gives you creative ideas for solutions to problems, that warns you of potential trouble ahead. The books are all about how to tell the difference or how to make peace with the inner critic.

I agree that people are hearing these, I just think it's better to call them what the Bible calls them – demons and the Holy Spirit. If it were your own voice, it would not react the way it does when questioned directly about Jesus Christ. I John 4:2 says that "no spirit of antichrist can acknowledge that Jesus Christ came in the flesh." You ask your "inner critic" to acknowledge that Jesus Christ came in the flesh and you just might be shocked at how truly mean your "inner critic" is. In fact, it's not even you at all!

I don't teach people to make peace with their inner critic. I teach people how to put on the armor of God, take the sword of Truth – and slice that nasty thing to shreds. I teach people how to walk in their inheritance as daughters and sons of the Most High God, how to access the Armory of the Lord (Jeremiah 50:25) and start shredding everything that is holding them captive to sin, fear, doubt, loneliness, lust, anger, unforgiveness, bitterness, hate, envy, greed or anything else. I take seriously the instruction of Isaiah 58:

Isaiah 58:6-12 – [Is] not this the fast that I have chosen? to loose the bands of wickedness, to undo the heavy burdens, and to let the oppressed go free, and that ye break every yoke? [Is it] not to deal thy bread to the hungry, and that thou bring the poor that are cast out to thy house? when thou seest the naked, that thou cover him; and that thou hide not thyself from thine own flesh? Then shall thy light break forth as the morning, and thine health shall spring forth speedily: and thy righteousness shall go before thee; the glory of the LORD shall be thy reward. Then shalt thou call, and the LORD shall answer; thou shalt cry, and he shall say, Here I [am]. If thou take away from the midst of thee the yoke, the putting forth of the finger, and speaking vanity; And [if] thou draw out thy soul to the hungry, and satisfy the afflicted soul; then shall thy light rise in obscurity, and thy darkness [be] as the noonday: And the LORD shall guide thee continually, and satisfy thy soul in drought, and make fat thy bones: and thou shalt be like a watered garden, and like a spring of water, whose waters fail not. And [they that shall be] of thee shall build the old waste places: thou shalt raise up the foundations of many generations; and thou shalt be called, The repairer of the breach, The restorer of paths to dwell in.

Wouldn't that be nice? All we have to do is get them free and pour ourselves out? Do you have the slightest idea how to do that? We do. And it works.

WHY MUST WE DEAL WITH IT?

Well, you should be getting a flavor of it by now, but there's more to this. It's not just that a Dad Filter can bind you up from receiving healing or deliverance because you don't think Dad will help you in a time of need, it's much deeper than that. In the Case Studies chapter I try to illustrate just a few of the various possible flavors and effects of this. But one of the really critical things to think about is the warning of Jesus that we might not inherit the Kingdom of God unless we come to Him like a little child. And I don't think coming to Him like a suspicious, cynical, abused, fearful little child is what He had in mind.

> Matthew 18:1-6 – At the same time came the disciples unto Jesus, saying, Who is the greatest in the kingdom of heaven? And Jesus called a little child unto him, and set him in the midst of them, And said, Verily I say unto you, Except ye be converted, and become as little children, ye shall not enter into the kingdom of heaven. Whosoever

therefore shall humble himself as this little child, the same is greatest in the kingdom of heaven. And whoso shall receive one such little child in my name receiveth me. But whoso shall offend one of these little ones which believe in me, it were better for him that a millstone were hanged about his neck, and [that] he were drowned in the depth of the sea.

Mark 10:15 – Verily I say unto you , Whosoever shall not receive the kingdom of God as a little child, he shall not enter therein.

Luke 18:17 – Verily I say unto you, Whosoever shall not receive the kingdom of God as a little child shall in no wise enter therein.

I don't think He's kidding. To repeat it in three different Gospels seems like it might be important. I know that when the Lord was refining me, He was having me lay down all kinds of things. I must decrease so that He can increase. He says that our flesh must be crucified daily. I would beg Him to kill all of me, just get me out completely, leave nothing but Christ in me. Let me just be a meat puppet with nothing left of me.

He said, "No. I love you. I made you special. I'm not going to kill all of you."

"Well, Lord, you're sure killing big chunks of me for loving me so much! What's going to be left when you're finished killing everything?"

He said, "I'm going to kill everything that's more than about six years old. All I need from you is, 'My Dad can beat up your Dad.'"

And He's pretty well done it. And I'm grateful. All He needs from us is faith like a child. That kind of David and Goliath faith that just KNOWS that Dad has got your back. Along the way, He had to deal with my own Dad Filter that I didn't know I had. (More on that under Case Studies.)

It's not just that this keeps us from receiving all that we are due as joint heirs – ultimately, that would be a humanistic, hedonistic, selfish reason to deal with this. No, it's not that simple. The biggest reason to do something about this is that He is a Dad that loves you desperately, longs to pull you up on His lap and kiss your boo-boos and come through for you. He wants to prove His love for you and He wants you to lean on Him.

No, the best reason to deal with this and get rid of this filter is because it grieves God every second that we hold Him at arms length because we think He's like <u>that</u> guy. That He's out to get us, that He's a judgemental, angry, vengeful, unstable jerk. Or that He's so important and so busy that we shouldn't bother Him and it's enough to know that He's out there somewhere. Or that He's only for emergencies when the car breaks down or we need bail money or something. Or that He's so small that we're smarter than Him and whatever His plans are, we can improve on them 'cause we've been around.

No, the right thing is to get it out of the way because it's a lie. It's a lie we've believed and repeated. And all liars will burn in the lake of fire with the abominable and the murders and thieves and the rest. Why would you want to hold onto a lie? Fear of the Lord is the beginning of wisdom. That doesn't mean terror of the Lord, that means AWE for who He truly is, for how big He is and still loves you like He does.

Do you understand that part of the message of Communion is that Jesus entered a blood covenant, became blood brothers with us. That means that when your village is attacked, my village will come help. That all my warriors and all my people are your people. That whatever I have is at your disposal and we are bonded for life. Every time you take Communion, it's a renewal of your blood oath that He would shed His blood for you and you're expected to shed your blood for Him if it's necessary.

Why would the King of the Universe, the creator of all things, the breather of stars, have His only son offer up all His stuff to YOU when you have nothing?! What kind of strategic alliance is this? Is you village really going to go defend <u>Him</u>? Do you really have anything at all? How does this make any sense? Why would He make a contract like that with someone who has nothing? How more lop-sided can a deal be?

That is what the Love of God is all about. That is what Jesus offered and what we receive as Joint Heirs with Christ. That is what we're NOT accessing because we can't get our heads around it and we're too obsessed with the fake little pleasures and temptations on this nasty mud-ball of a planet.

One time we were having a Bible study out in the park. I was getting everything set up and I asked the Lord a question. Now, I normally just ask (in my head) what the Lord wants me to do and leave it to them to sort out who is going to answer me. I've heard all three – Father, Son and Holy Spirit – and I know they are three, yet they are one. This isn't the place for a discussion about the Trinity, but I know that the Oneness Pentecostals that say that Jesus is the Father, the Son and the Holy Spirit are wrong. And I know that the people that seem to worship the Holy Spirit are wrong. And I know that the Son came to bring all glory and honor to the Father. He came to be Jacob's Ladder to connect us to Father God, not for us to live on the ladder.

Anyway, I asked the Lord a question and I heard Jesus answer me and He said, "I can't help you with that. You're going to have to ask our Dad."

Well, I just stopped dead in my tracks! I mean, I know all the verses about joint heirs and sitting on Jesus' throne as He sits on the Father's throne and all, but I'd never been face to face with the reality of Jesus Christ, the Prince of Peace, the Spotless Lamb of God, the Lion of Judah, saying, "OUR Dad," to me! I don't even remember what the question was, I just stood there with my head spinning, "Oh, man! My Dad, His Dad, our Dad! Oh, wow! Joint heirs, equal time, love all the kids the same. Zowie!" (I think I actually said, "Zowie." That's how far gone I was.)

Do you have any conception of that? Do you have any idea what it means to be totally overwhelmed by everything coming at you and cry out, "Daddy! Please help!" to the

Almighty Creator of All Things? I pray that you would get it. I pray that this book would do something to your heart to get it to sink in and stay there forever. You can't walk right with Him without allowing Him to be Dad to you in whatever way HE wants to be Dad to you. Maybe you need a spanking – He knows best. Maybe you need a hug – He knows best.

I can tell you this. My life is unbelievably hard. People that live here with us can tell you that they don't know anybody that could do what I do and cope with all the things I cope with. By all accounts I should have had a mental breakdown a long time ago! The level of spiritual warfare, raw naked hatred from people, betrayal, money problems, not to mention the daily requirements of housing 50-70 people and feeding 5,000 per month. People coming to me because someone used their Worcestershire sauce in the fridge without permission, people having accidents in the ministry van, roommate conflicts, zoning fights with the city and so much more. I can tell you that there are a bunch of times that the Father pulled me up onto His lap and rubbed my head and whispered sweet things to me and it was as REAL as this book you're holding. As real as anything I know to be real. I've felt His hand on my shoulder. I've felt Him rubbing my head and wiping my tears. Without Him being the Dad that I know He is to me, I would never survive all that I'm called to do. And I'm just getting starting!! There is SO much more to do!

If it's not enough that you need to deal with this because you're not getting healed or blessed; if it's not enough that you need to deal with this because it's a lie; then deal with it because He loves you, knew you from your mother's womb,

36

designed you from before the creation of the universe, sent His only Son to die for you so that you could be reconciled to Him – and desperately wants to swoop in and hug the stuffing out of you and push you on the swings and take care of all your problems.

Even the Bible says so. What He wants from you is very simple. (In **bold**.)

Psalm 50: 1-23 –The mighty God, [even] the LORD, hath spoken, and called the earth from the rising of the sun unto the going down thereof. Out of Zion, the perfection of beauty, God hath shined. Our God shall come, and shall not keep silence: a fire shall devour before him, and it shall be very tempestuous round about him. He shall call to the heavens from above, and to the earth, that he may judge his people.

"Gather my saints together unto me; those that have made a covenant with me by sacrifice."

And the heavens shall declare his righteousness: for God [is] judge himself. Selah.

"Hear, O my people, and I will speak; O Israel, and I will testify against thee: I [am] God, [even] thy God. I will not reprove thee for thy sacrifices or thy burnt offerings, [to have been] continually before me. I will take no bullock out of thy house, [nor] he goats out of thy folds. For every beast of the forest [is] mine, [and] the cattle upon a thousand hills. I know all the fowls of the mountains: and the wild beasts of the field [are] mine. If I were hungry, I would not tell thee: for the world [is] mine, and the fulness thereof. Will I eat the flesh of bulls, or drink the blood of goats?

Offer unto God thanksgiving; and pay thy vows unto the most High: And call upon me in the day of trouble: I will deliver thee, and thou shalt glorify me.

But unto the wicked God saith, What hast thou to do to declare my statutes, or [that] thou shouldest take my covenant in thy mouth? Seeing thou hatest instruction, and castest my words behind thee. When thou sawest a thief, then thou consentedst with him, and hast been partaker with adulterers. Thou givest thy mouth to evil, and thy tongue frameth deceit. Thou sittest [and] speakest against thy brother; thou slanderest thine own mother's son. These [things] hast thou done, and I kept silence; thou thoughtest that I was altogether [such an one] as thyself: [but] I will reprove thee, and set [them] in order before thine eyes. Now consider this, ye that forget God, lest I tear [you] in pieces, and [there be] none to deliver.

Whoso offereth praise glorifieth me: and to him that ordereth [his] conversation [aright] will I shew the salvation of God."

There are so many beautiful promises, so many places where you can clearly see what a sweet, patient, loving Dad He really is. Let me give you some more reasons.

Luke 15:11-31 – And he said, A certain man had two sons: And the younger of them said to his father, Father, give me the portion of goods that falleth to me. And he divided unto them his living. And not many days after the younger son gathered all together, and took his journey into a far country, and there wasted his substance with riotous living. And when he had spent all, there arose a mighty famine in that land; and he began to be in want. And he went and joined himself to a citizen of that country; and he sent him into his fields to feed swine. And he would fain have filled his belly with the husks that the swine did eat: and no man gave unto him. And when he came to himself, he said, How many hired servants of my father's have bread enough and to spare, and I perish with hunger! I will arise and go to my father, and will say unto him, Father, I have sinned against heaven, and before thee, And am no more worthy to be called thy son: make me as one of thy hired servants.

And he arose, and came to his father. But when he was yet a great way off, his father saw him, and had compassion, and ran, and fell on his neck, and kissed him. And the son said unto him, Father, I have sinned against heaven, and in thy sight, and am no more worthy to be called thy son. But the father said to his servants, Bring forth the best robe, and put it on him; and put a ring on his hand, and shoes on his feet. And bring hither the fatted calf, and kill it; and let us eat, and be merry: For this my son was dead, and is alive again; he was lost, and is found. And they began to be merry.

Now his elder son was in the field: and as he came and drew nigh to the house, he heard musick and dancing. And he called one of the servants, and asked what these things meant. And he said unto him, Thy brother is come; and thy father hath killed the fatted calf, because he hath received him safe and sound. And he was angry, and would not go in: therefore came his father out, and intreated him. And he answering said to his father, Lo, these many years do I serve thee, neither transgressed I at any time thy commandment: and yet thou never gavest me a kid, that I might make merry with my friends: But as soon as this thy son was come, which hath devoured thy living with harlots, thou hast killed for him the fatted calf. And he said unto him, Son, thou art ever with me, and all that I have is thine. It was meet that we should make merry, and be glad: for this thy brother was dead, and is alive again; and was lost, and is found.

May I just try for a moment to explain to you how radical this story is? This is part of a series of parables that start with, "The kingdom of God is like…" These are efforts to explain to the people what Father God is like and what acquiring the kingdom is worth.

This story is addressed to scribes and Pharisees, the religious leaders, known for their ultra-conservative, fundamentalist views (and hard-heartedness). You have to understand that Jewish law says that if a son is rebellious and a drunkard, you're supposed to stone him!

Deuteronomy 21:18-21 – If a man have a stubborn and rebellious son, which will not obey the voice of his father, or the voice of his mother, and [that], when they have chastened him, will not hearken unto them: Then shall his father and his mother lay hold on him, and bring him out unto the elders of his city, and unto the gate of his place; And they shall say unto the elders of his city, This our son

[is] stubborn and rebellious, he will not obey our voice; [he is] a glutton, and a drunkard. And all the men of his city shall stone him with stones, that he die: so shalt thou put evil away from among you; and all Israel shall hear, and fear.

Now in this story, the son goes to the father and says, "I wish you were dead. I want my inheritance now!" So immediately, you would see these Pharisees bristle at the very idea of a son speaking to a father like that! Then Jesus goes on and tells them that the Father gives him his share of everything! Well, that's just unheard of! Then this Jewish kid goes into a Gentile land and wastes all the money on riotous living and harlots!

OK, now Jesus is really pushing their buttons. If you think we have a race relations problem in the United States, you have NO idea what it was like at the time of Jesus. The Jews hated the Gentiles like nothing we've ever seen. If the shadow of a Gentile touched you, you were unclean. If a Gentile drank out of a cup of yours, there was no way to clean it enough, you just had to destroy it. They were filthy, disgusting, heathen, swine-eaters that should get out of Israel or die. Even the Samaritans – who were like cousins – were hated because they weren't pure enough! Now this kid took his dad's wealth and is wasting it whoring around with the Gentiles. The crowd listening to Jesus would be outraged! (He's quite an engaging story-teller.)

Now the story gets interesting. A famine hits that nasty Gentile land (Hurray!). And the rotten brat kid runs out of money and no one will help him (Hurray!). So he hires on with a man that sets him to slopping the pigs (Right ON! Serves him right!) You can almost see the Pharisees grinning about God's justice on this kid. Jews wouldn't allow pigs anywhere near them. They don't eat pig, they don't raise pigs, they don't touch pigs, and they don't like anybody that does. And here this kid is starving and having to eat the corn cobs and stuff that even the pigs won't eat! The Pharisees are practically rooting for the pigs!

Then the kid realizes that even his fathers servants eat better. Maybe he should go home, throw himself on his father's mercy and offer to be a hired servant. So he heads for home. While he's still a long way off, the Father sees him coming down the road and runs to him, throws himself on him and hugs him and kisses him! At this point the Pharisees are probably just beside themselves. Who would do that?

The son speaks forth one of the simplest purest confessions in the Bible, "Father, I have sinned against heaven, and in thy sight, and am no more worthy to be called thy son." That about covers it all, doesn't it? Who among is is really worthy to be called God's son? Only Jesus. Starting with a confession like that is always a good start.

This boy had some expectations about his Dad. He knew him well enough to know he wouldn't get stoned for demanding his inheritance. That says something about Dad. He knew that his Dad would probably at least let him stay as a hired hand – that's something. But somewhere he probably also thought that Dad was a dud, a pushover, and that the fun was "out there somewhere."

But I'm pretty sure that he didn't expect this. The Father throws himself at the rotten brat, tells the servants to get a robe and shoes and put a ring (sign of authority and sonship) on his finger, kill the best calf and get ready for a party. This is probably pushing all the buttons of the Pharisees! You can almost see their jaws hanging open. But then Jesus doubles-down and pokes them right in the eye.

Because at home the whole time was the elder brother who was doing his duty, being religious about his work, serving like a good son. But is resentful that this rotten stinker, this wasteful, selfish, sinning, little brother of his has blown the family's wealth and not been here helping out on the farm and the Father is rejoicing over it! (Do you see that by taking him back as a son, the Father is acknowledging his rights of inheritance and wiping the slate clean, so now the remaining estate would be divided again between the two brothers!)

This is a direct frontal assault on the Pharisees and their uppity attitude and resistance to seeing Christ come for sinners when they Pharisees have been there all along doing the "right thing." Jesus tries to show them what the love of the Father is like, how merciful, how forgiving – and how those that thought they were obeying aren't clean either because they did it with a wrong heart and resent the will of the Father. Who are you to demand that HE do things YOUR way?

I hope I'm getting through to you here. If you're not seeing God for the fullness of who He is, then you're in some foreign land slopping the pigs – to some degree or another.

Nothing compares to having a right relationship with Father God. The author C. S. Lewis said that we all have a "God-shaped void" that nothing else can fill. Well, I disagree with him on a bunch of stuff – and I disagree with him on this. I think we all have a "Daddy God-shaped void." I don't think it's enough to fill that void with a deity, I think what we long for, what so many people are desperate for is a right relationship with a Heavenly Father.

I can tell you this. I just know that I don't care if it's a ten lane highway with trucks going 90 miles an hour, I know that I know that I know that if I step off the curb, if I'm holding my Heavenly Father's hand, I'm going to get safely to the other side. I didn't always used to feel that way, but I begged Him to show me who He is and He answered. He's a great Dad that pals around with me, that disciplines me at times, that blesses me at times, that protects me, that guides my paths and that loves me more than I can ever explain to anyone. He has sacrificed for me in ways that I can't even get my head around.

I wish you could know Him that way – and more. I pray you will. I know He wants you to. He's desperate to swoop in and hug you and fix everything. Will you let Him?

Who would you rather listen to?

YOU say:	It's impossible.
GOD says:	All things are possible. (Luke18:27)
YOU say:	I'm exhausted.
GOD says:	I will give you rest. (Matthew 11:28-30)
YOU say:	I'm not able.
GOD says:	I am able. (II Corinthians 9:8)
YOU say:	It's not worth it.
GOD says:	It will be worth it. (Romans 8:28)
YOU say:	Nobody loves me.
GOD says:	I love you. (John 2: 16 and John 13:34)
YOU say:	I can't keep going.
GOD says:	My Grace is sufficient for you. (II Corinthians 12:9 and Psalm 91:15)
YOU say:	I don't know what to do.
GOD says:	I will direct your steps. (Proverbs 3: 5-6)
YOU say:	I can't do it.
GOD says:	You can do all things. (Philippians 4:13)
YOU say:	I can't forgive myself.
GOD says:	I forgive you (I John 1:9 and Romans 8:1)
YOU say:	I don't have enough faith.
GOD says:	I've given everyone a measure of faith. (Romans 12:3)

YOU say: I'm not smart enough.
GOD says: I will give you wisdom. (I Corinthians 1:30)

YOU say: I can't survive.
GOD says: I will supply all your needs. (Philippians 4:19)

YOU say: I'm afraid.
GOD says: I didn't give you a spirit of fear. (II Tim. 1:7)

YOU say: I'm worried.
GOD says: Cast all your cares on me. (I Peter 5:7)

YOU say: I feel all alone.
God says: I will never leave you or forsake you.
            (Hebrews 13:5)

YOU say: I'm in danger.
GOD says: I will keep you from harm. (Psalm 121:7)

YOU say: I don't think God hears me.
GOD says: Before you call I will hear you. (Isaiah 65:24)

YOU say: I think God is out to get me.
GOD says: I long to be gracious to you. (Isaiah 30:18)

YOU say: I think God has given up on me.
GOD says: I have redeemed you. You're mine. (Isa. 43:1)

YOU say: I'm not sure I'm saved.
GOD says: He who believes has eternal life. (John 6:47)

CASE STUDIES

The most obvious Dad Filter would be the one where a person grew up with no Dad at all, so they have basically no relationship with God. OK, maybe He's out there somewhere, but so far away it makes no difference. This kind of person is typically going to rely on themselves and do too much in their own power.

Case Study 1 – Doug (Me) – Smarter than God

In all the other case studies, I've changed the names and personal details so as not to violate any confidentiality. But this one is about me. This is my effort to be transparent and show you how subtle this can be. If you were reading the book carefully and have any kind of retention at all, you'll remember me saying on page <u>one</u> that I was twice as smart as my Earth Dad. Well, I didn't mean that as hyperbole. I knew when I was thirteen years old that I was smarter than him. And I don't mean that in a smart-aleck-teenager-sure-he's-got-the-world-by-the-tail sort of a way. I mean it in a test scores, reading seminary texts when I was in 8th grade, Dad writes a book and I'll edit it for him sort of a way. Never mind the blinking 12:00 on the VCR that he had no idea what to do with. There was just sort of a knowing that I could pretty well handle whatever. I always had people coming to me for advice, and thanking me for the wisdom of it.

My Dad (Bob), recently commented to me on a strange incident that always stuck with him. I was about thirteen and he got a call from a grown woman asking for me. I stood in the hall (back in the day when phones weren't cordless) and talked with her for over an hour. When I got off the phone, he said, "Who was that?" I said, "Oh, that was Mrs. Stone, my English teacher." "Are you having trouble in school?" he said. "Oh, no," I casually replied, "She's just going through a divorce and needed someone to talk to." I didn't think anything of it, but as a pastor and counselor, it just blew his mind that a forty year old woman would call me for advice!

Well, this grew and grew over the years. Something snapped the day Dad and I were wrestling in the front yard for the upteenth time and I figured out how to beat him. Something dies inside when a kid learns that Dad isn't as indestructible as they thought. We never wrestled any more after that.

In 2005 at my furniture store when God was sending people for ministry and telling us about demons and Dad Filters and all kinds of things, we were all trying to navigate how to BE the Church and walk this out. We kept hearing from the Lord what His plan was, then I would edit it, make some improvements and implement it. And it would go badly.

A brother loved me enough to get up in my face and say boldly, "I'm sick and tired of God telling us to do something and you tweaking it and people getting hurt."

"I don't do that."

"Yes, you do. I think you have a Dad Filter."

"I don't have a Dad Filter," I whined.

"How many times have I heard you tell people how you were smarter than Earth Dad? I think you think you're smarter than God."

"No, I don't." I reply sheepishly.

"Would you just shut up and ask God?" he retorted.

"Uh, Lord? Do I have a Dad Filter and I think I'm smarter than you." I pray fearfully.

"Yep. You do," came the instant (and totally believable) reply from the Almighty.

"OH!! No way!! What the heck!! That's so gross! Really! How? That's like antichrist in the extreme! That I would seriously think I'm smarter than YOU?! Oh, God, that's horrible! I'm so sorry! Please forgive me! I get it. I did it. I admit. Please crush it. I'm little, You're big. I'm a grasshopper. I'm sorry I ever thought that I could improve on your plans. Please beat it out of me and ignore any suggestions I make." And some good crying ensued.

Do you see? There are all kinds of ways to put The Almighty Father in a box. Without knowing I'd done it, I put Him in a box shaped like Earth Dad – a box that allowed me to feel superior to God. Pitiful. The reality is that it doesn't matter what Man, no matter how good or smart or loving, that you use as a model for that box – it's always going to be too small. So I asked God to teach me how to stop trying to help. And while there are still some struggles occasionally against my flesh (or brain) that wants to help Him out, mostly I do a pretty good job now of letting Him run things His way – and it's not the way I would EVER do things! But it all works out far better in the end.

Case Study 2 – Jennifer – No Fear of the Lord

It can be all different flavors. One sister that I counseled with was the youngest child of eight, with seven older brothers. She was the princess of the family, always got what she wanted. She had her dad tied around her little finger. She was always pampered, he never raised a hand to her, never said a harsh word to her. She could not get her head around fear of the Lord. She understood Abba Father, push me on the swings, kiss my boo-boos really well – but she couldn't have a complete relationship with Father God because she didn't understand wrath and anger and justice. She just believed that whatever she would ask for she should get. Then she ends up in this strange dissonance situation because sometimes she asks the Father for things, doesn't get them and doesn't know how to process that at all – because Dad's just give you whatever you want. When there is sickness or illness or suffering or family death, she can't process it, because God is not like that, God wouldn't do that. Well, yes, He is. Is God love? Yes. He's also justice. He has to be both. There's no love if there's no justice. There has to be punishment, there has to be reward.

If you decide that God is love, God isn't mad at anybody, God just loves you, that He'll never discipline you that He's just soft and fluffy, then you've got an entirely one-sided God there that you're worshiping and it may not be the real God at all – because He's way bigger than that, way more complicated.

Case Study 3 – Edith – Dad's just using you.

One of the most dramatic (or saddest) counseling sessions I had was with a sister in her 70's. Despite being married for 50 years, she had never had a man really express to her that she was valuable and loved and needed. Her husband was cold and distant and that's all she ever expected – in fact, more likely she held him at a distance because of her filters. She had served the Lord all her life. Had been a missionary, a music director, Sunday School teacher and more. She loved God and served Him – out of raw, naked fear.

I knew she had lots of things binding her up, but the Lord would not allow me to address any of them before dealing with her Dad Filter. So I ask her to tell me about her dad. Well, it turns out that he was a very high level Freemason (and I don't have time to talk about all the spiritual dangers of Freemasonry here, but know that it <u>will</u> bring generational curses down on your family and it's basically worshiping satan). There was a practicing witch down the road that had promised her father that the crops on his farm would grow well if he would bring his only daughter down to her house every so often. Then this witch (white/black, there's no difference, either you're for Jesus or you're on the other side) would hypnotize her while staring through the flame of a candle, take her clothes off, lay her on a stone slab, perform ceremonies and do all kinds of things to her.

For a number of years in her early teens she remembers going down to the witch's house, although many of the details are a blur. To that day every time she closed her eyes, she could still see that witch staring at her through that candle. As she is talking, everything in me wants to reach out in time and grab this father by the scruff of the neck and shake him like a rag doll.

She loved her father and didn't want to hear that he was a bad man. She was stuck in "Dad is Superman" mode and believed fully that it was just her fault or something that needed to be done and he was right. All I can hear the Father saying is that this man offered his only child to Molech (look it up in the Bible, Leviticus 20 and elsewhere) and God is SERIOUSLY furious about it.

Occasionally, the Lord will have me do something that any "normal" Christian counselor wouldn't expect at all. So I tell her, "God thinks your dad was a big jerk. And God was furious for what he did to you. And God got even with him." Now, at that point I have no idea what happened, I just know what the Lord said. She goes on to tell me how he died of a horrible, terrible stomach cancer that ate him from the inside. She believed the witch died in a car accident.

So I ask the Lord if we can crush the Dad Filter. He says, "No." "Well, why not?" "Because you have to deal with the unforgiveness first."

Now would be a good time to mention that the Dad Filter doesn't stand alone as the worst thing that will clog you up and bind up healing and blessing and growth. Deeper still is unforgiveness. We're going to hit this a couple of times in these Case Studies to emphasize this.

So I say, "Lord, who is the unforgiveness toward?"

"The dad."

So we talk about it, I show her how God was there all along, how angry He was, how He defended her and got justice for her – and how this is still live, it is still a doorway for the enemy because of the unforgiveness in her heart toward Earth Dad. She confesses that deep down, under the effort to convince herself that Dad was Superman and have the "politically correct" attitude about Dad, was a seething rage for what he'd done. She is a little too proper to give it voice, so I describe for her how God feels about this wicked, wretch of a human being. She acknowledges her anger, acknowledges that she needs to release it, asks the Lord to take it – and He does. She cries a little and feels it lift.

Then the Lord says, "Now the witch."

OK, well, it's not like I ever thought this job would be easy, but that's a tall order!

So we talk about it. She sees that the Lord has already settled it. But she's still seeing the eyes of this witch all the time because of her own unforgiveness. This is live ammo that should have been defused a long time ago, but she herself is keeping it alive. And it's not like she was walking around every day fuming about this, it was buried deep and stored away, but still allowed the enemy legal ground to mess with her because there was unforgiveness in her heart. Biblically speaking, I'm not sure she could be saved so long as that was there. If you don't forgive others, God won't forgive you. So satan wants to keep it there buried deep, as a loophole to use against you at the final judgement. So we gave it to the Lord and she released it, and He took it and she was free.

The Lord said, "Now you can deal with the Dad Filter."

So we talked about how she had been serving God out of fear and she'd never once heard God say anything kind or affirming or sweet to her. She agreed that it was her fault and that she had put Him in a box. She said she was sorry and we cried together and she smashed that lens, that filter up into a million pieces. But it's not enough to get the bad out, we have to get the good replacement IN. And I have a lot of really good "Dad stuff" in my cup, so I put my arm around her and held her hand and told her that whatever I had, whatever the Lord had done to me so that I could hear Him and sit on His lap and know Him as Daddy, I would give to her – even if I never got it back. And I meant it.

And we prayed and I could feel the "dunamis" going out of my cup. And after about fifteen minutes, I kind of wanted to pat her and tell her that was enough, but Father God was yelling at me and threatening what He would do if I so much as tried to cut her off.

"I've been waiting 74 years to give her a hug!! You're my hands and feet, just love her and let her rest in my arms as long as she wants. She has to learn that I'm never going to pull away from her until SHE pulls away from ME!"

How do you argue with that? So we sat there. Thirty minutes. Forty-five minutes. An hour. I think she took a nap snuggled up into my shoulder with her head on my chest. And I knew there was this mature, proper woman in her thinking, "You know, this is quite an imposition. This probably doesn't look good. We really should be getting back on the road now." But the little girl in her was screaming, "SCREW THAT!! I NEED A HUG!!" And the little girl won. (And I'm glad she did.)

And it wasn't just me either, the sister that drove her up three hours to meet with me is sitting across from us, looking at her watch and calculating how late they are – and God is telling her to shut her mouth and keep out of it and not to dare try to stop this.

At about an hour and a half, she let go of me. And she was different. She was free. And she heard God tell her all kinds of sweet things and tell her what He had in mind for their relationship going forward. It was an honor to be the hug of the Father and to see Him fight for His little ones.

Case Study 4 – Anne – Drunk Marine Drill Instructor

Not all the Case Studies are success stories. Anne grew up with a father who was an alcoholic, womanizing, ex-Marine drill instructor. When she was between seven and twelve years old, she would remember him coming home from the bars, throwing things, screaming at her mother, and occasionally hitting her. While Anne was never abused physically, she vividly recalled a time when she came home from school and hadn't done the dishes before he got home and while she was in the kitchen trying to do them quickly, he screamed at her until she wet her pants. She was terrified of him.

One of the ugliest, most selfish things I've heard was that when he would come home after drinking, the parents would scream and throw things at each other until he passed out – while the poor girl hid under the covers or under the bed. When he passed out her mother would come in and get her out of bed and hold her on her lap and rock her, to make HERSELF feel better. All the while this kid is just wide-eyed and terrified by it all.

At about seven years old she got a younger sister with special needs. At about twelve years old, Dad finally divorced and took off – rarely around and rarely paying child support (or so the story goes). Mom became a single bread-winner, Anne became a latchkey kid and caregiver for the younger sister. In some ways, she became the replacement dad in the system. Later on, she'd be molested by the neighbor boys. Mom dated multiple guys and eventually settled on one who had money and who she could control.

The result is a layered "onion" of filters from Dad and Mom and circumstances and other people in her life. Mom insisted that all men were pigs, that all they wanted was sex and there was no pleasure in it for the women. She learned that Dad's are out to get you, they're a terror and you're better off without them. She learned that you have to do everything yourself and you can't wait on somebody to do it for you. She learned that if one guy doesn't work out for you, you should dump him and go find someone who is more compliant.

Because of all this she projected onto men that they were pigs, expected to be abandoned, saw sex as dirty, and had to control everything and everyone around her so that she wouldn't be in an out of control situation ever again. With God she expected that the slightest misstep would result in horrible consequences. If she missed Sunday School, that lump in her breast was probably going to be malignant. She had mammograms nearly annually and was often on the internet looking for what exotic disease might be the cause of the new ache she just developed. She was on anti-depressants and anti-anxiety meds for many years.

We tried repeatedly to address the filters of all kinds. She couldn't trust the Lord to defend her, she had to do it herself. She couldn't trust the Lord to heal her, she had to take medicine. She couldn't have a right relationship with people because as soon as they disagreed with her, she would write them off and sever contact. She would read the Bible, so long as it was only passages that reinforced her decisions. When confronted with any passages to the contrary, she would reason them away or deny them outright or cut the person off.

I continue to pray that someday she will see clearly. Under it all is a little kid that still hasn't made peace and forgiven and let it go. Her relationship is with a god of her own making that rubber stamps whatever she wants. There is no sin in her life because there is no conviction from god for anything that she does – because god agrees with her on everything. And it is a god of her own making.

Case Study 5 – Cindy – No love.

In 2007 we had a revival meeting at a community center in a little town just North of Kansas City and people came from all over. A dear sister brought a friend of hers to the event, Cindy, who really needed to get free. I'd met her briefly before and had a grasp on the fundamental problem.

She worked at a fast food restaurant in the drive-thru. She was kind of plain and a little overweight, and she wore lots of makeup and all kinds of buttons and flowers and smiley face pins. She was known and liked for her happy disposition and how she made people smile. The restaurant didn't mind that she kind of looked like a clown, because it made people happy and they liked driving up to her window. But the reality was that it was all a desperate effort to get someone, anyone to be nice to her. She had labored on this "look" more and more over the years to try harder and harder to make people smile. The thing was, they weren't smiling so much because they loved her, but because she was sort of humiliating herself and they found it funny.

When we started digging, it was clear there was a huge critical spirit (self-condemnation), a fear, a despair and a really old, really deep loneliness. As we got to talking, despite saying all the right things and years in "church," she couldn't ever remember a time when she heard God speak to her in any way. She knew that God is love and she tells people that, but she doesn't believe God loves her. Guess what? Earth Dad also was distant and aloof and never praised her, never said he loved her, never showed her any affection at all. In fact, no man in her life EVER had told her she was pretty. Even her husband basically let her do whatever so long as food was on the table and she had a job. Her kids treated her like hired help. Now, I'm sure that the husband wasn't a bad guy, but a filter like this is going to attract people into your life to treat you badly (because you think it's what you deserve), or will train the people in your life (who might otherwise treat you well) that they can take advantage of you because you expect them to.

We identified the Dad Filter, she saw it, but couldn't fathom the idea of calling Almighty God something personal and intimate and informal like "Daddy." Dads are big and scary and nothing you do will please them and they just tolerate you as a necessary evil. She was sure that she was a failure and a disappointment to everyone in her life. She looked in the mirror and always saw something that needed to be hidden. She chose a fake smile and colorful buttons.

There is no real, true cure for loneliness other than a right relationship with Father God and teaching people how to hold His hand every day. No person, no car, no job, no money, no food, no drug will satisfy that loneliness. She was desperate.

We talked to her about it, even pounded her with Bible verses about His love, even showed her how prideful it was to believe that you were SO bad that God's love could reach everyone but you. But she just could not get it in her head or heart what a good Dad might be like. She had no context at all. So she repented for binding God, knew she'd done it and felt sorry and we crushed the Filter. But the only way to impress upon her who God really was as a Dad and how much He wanted to swoop in and love her was to impart it to her or beg that God would do it Himself. I have a picture here somewhere of Sarah holding Cindy's hands and praying SO hard for her. We both held her hands and prayed that any good thing we had that would help would be given to Cindy. After breaking lots of things and "pushing" really hard (prayers of intercession) for about a half hour, all of a sudden she bursts into tears, looks up at me smiling and says, "God said I was pretty!"

The Lord said to go outside, so we went out the back of the community center and walked across the grass toward the playground equipment. She pranced. I don't know if you can get a visual on that, but she was barely touching the ground, spinning and leaping a little and frolicking like a little girl with ribbons in her hair just wanting to see her skirt spin around. She kept saying, "God loves me! God thinks I'm pretty!" And the Lord told me to take her to the playground and push her on the swings for awhile. It was beautiful!

Case Study 6 – Monique – Never around.

Another example of the supernatural solution to these problems was with Monique, a young lady getting ready to start college. I had received some family background previously, as her mother had been here to get some counseling and we talked through the problems with her own father – and now husband – that were distant and aloof. She had brought one of her daughters here to counsel with me.

We talked about the fundamentals of the Dad Filter and she agreed that her relationship with God was cold and distant, with very little interaction. But she loved the Lord and was really seeing Him try to overcome the walls she'd built up against getting close to Him. He was making efforts to show her what a good Dad He could be, but there were still things in the way. Fundamentally she just couldn't get her head around what it would even be like to have a good Dad.

I told her about my own Earth Dad. How he was always there, how much he loved me, how he would sit in church with his arm around me and fiddle with my hair, how he put other things aside, how I knew that he would forgive anything and always be there for me. I cried a little and she could see how much I understand that my experience was rare and precious.

I told her about what my walk with Father God is like. About daily interaction and letting me rest my head on His chest and patting my head when I'm crying. About being there for me in every situation and getting me through things that nobody should be able to get through.

And I told her that I would be glad to give it all to her. I had had it for awhile and she needed it. And I meant it. So I held her hand and prayed, "Lord, she's sorry for putting you in a box. She confessed it, Lord. Please forgive her and fill her with every good thing. Whatever I have, give it to her. Whatever is holy and pure and true and helps me to hear you and feel you and know how you feel about me, please give it to her, even if I never hear You again or feel you comfort me. Give it to her.

And I prayed a little and I could feel the "dunamis" leaving. (And please don't think I'm alone in this. We have LOTS of folks here that are really good at this. That's what we're about, teaching people what it's going to take to bring revival. All we need to do is stop praying for the Latter Rain and the Early Rain, stop praying for God to pour His Spirit out on all flesh – and go POUR His Spirit out on all flesh! He's waiting on US, not the other way around.) And she cried and I cried and God moved. After about fifteen minutes she let go of my hand, looked up and said, "I had a good dad."

"Huh?" I said, knowing that she, in fact, had a jerk dad.

She said, "I can't explain it, but my dad was there for me. He loves me. He came to my events and cheered for me."

Well, in fact, he didn't. But mine did. All she knew was that she could feel what a good dad was like and now she could relate to Father God better. Somehow, it transferred.

There are all kinds of congregations that believe in the gift of tongues – and people will go down front and they'll lay

God. The problem is that sometimes a "patient" is so covered in third-degree burns all over their body that there is just no way to hug them without causing them more pain. Some people would rather stick with the demons they know and the life they are used to, than risk it all on a better life they can't even imagine is possible.

Leslie was brought into a situation where Dad had left and Mom was homeless. At four years old she started being forced to perform oral sex on Mom. At eight years old she was being hired out as a prostitute. She started drinking at five years old and drugs and smoking came by nine years old.

Through this time her father was writing letters to her mom, but her mom was hiding them. Sometime in her preteen/early teens, Leslie found the letters and got in contact with Dad. She was desperate to escape a horrible situation and Dad invited her to come stay with him in another state.

Dad convinced her (through some twisted demon logic) that because she was his seed, she was who God had made to be a wife for him. Then follows rape, bondage and slavery to Dad. She was found chained behind Dad's business by a passerby who called the police. All of this before she could get a driver's license.

She was about forty when we met her and had been bouncing around for years, drawing welfare and doing what she had to do to survive. Whole chunks of her life were a blur because of the drugs and alcohol. We did all we could over the course of months to help her stay away from the alcohol. She knew that God had delivered her of the drugs and had stories of hearing Him and knowing that He loved her – but she couldn't believe it.

One of the strangest manifestations of this was that her personal worship time with the Lord often involved her having orgasms. She was absolutely convinced that it was Jesus, that it was pure, and that she was His Bride and that's just the way He wanted to relate to her. There was no talking her out of it. And yet, isn't it perfectly reasonable to expect when someone has learned their whole life that anyone close to you loves you because of your sexuality? She eventually took off when we started to get close to a break through. She was very much tortured by demons and was unwilling to really stand against them as she needed to. There were still unresolved issues with bitterness and unforgiveness – and likely many repressed memories that the enemy was still using as active gateways to maintain legal ground over her life. Truly a very sad case, but we have to trust that we did the best we could, that the seeds planted by the Lord will be watered by Him and that He is desperate to save her.

Even though I changed her name, the Lord knows who we're talking about. Please pray for her and for all of these people mentioned. Some will get it and hold on to it, and some will let the enemy steal it. We sow the seed, it's up to the Lord to bring the increase.

Case Study 8 – Fred – Unforgiveness.

Now, just to be transparent, 'Fred' is a composite. Fred is not a single individual person as we've described up until now. Fred is a collage, a collection, of people that we've counseled with over the years.

Fred's problem is that we can't do anything about his Dad Filter because of the unforgiveness in his heart. The we've talked earlier in this book about the danger of not forgiving others. The Bible says that God won't forgive you if you don't forgive them. But the very WORST kind of unforgiveness, the very most prideful and arrogant – and the best way to give satan lots of legal ground – is to have unforgiveness toward God.

Maybe Fred watched both of his parents commit suicide in front of him (we've seen that one). Maybe Fred and all his brothers and sisters were molested or viciously abused by Dad – and Mom just stood by and let it happen (we've seen that one). Maybe all of Fred's family were drunks and addicts and Fred grew up covered with scar tissue (we've seen that one).

Maybe when Fred was a kid he prayed and prayed for God to get him out of it and nothing seemed to have happened. Maybe Fred shook his little fist at God and said, "Why did You have me born into this family?!" Maybe Fred prayed for someone not to die, but they died anyway and Fred is really mad at God. In one way or another Fred wants God to pay for what He did to Fred.

The problem is, Fred is still standing. Fred doesn't see that God got him through – that Fred should be dead a hundred times over, but God stood by and deflected bullets and neutralized drug overdoses and drove the car when Fred was passed out drunk. All Fred knows is that all the problems he has are God's fault – and satan feeds that idea all the time.

It's one thing to not forgive a person – who is flawed and sinful and human. But to have unforgiveness in your heart toward GOD is just insanely prideful! Really? Have you looked up at the stars, Fred? Have you really considered for a moment that you know what's good for you better than the Almighty Creator of All Things. Do you really think that the God that knows the name of every star, every atom, every leaf, every snowflake, that THAT God somehow had it sneak past Him that you were getting pounded on? Like He wasn't right there? Like He wasn't stopping it from going too far? I don't care who you are or how badly you've been hurt, you're entirely barking up the wrong tree when you decide to take out all your bitterness and hurts on GOD.

The result is going to be a heart full of ugliness and bile and hatred. You can't just hate the Creator and then get along fine with all of His Creation. You're pretty well going to have to spit at everything and everybody in one way or another. Now, there's a fair chance that you didn't make this decision as an adult, that it was just something a kid decided on day when there was no one else to blame. Dad died, you're all alone. You can't blame Dad, he's a hero. You can't blame Mom, she's all you have left. So you blame God.

But you're a grown up now, Fred. You need to see how wrong-headed it was, how arrogant, how much like the snake in the Garden to think that YOU get to tell God how wrong He is and how YOU know best. That's just insane! So say you're sorry for the unforgiveness you've held in your heart (and nursed for years) toward God and tell Him that you may not get it, but He was right and you were wrong – and ask Him to scrub it all out of you.

How can you have a right relationship with Father God if you're sure He's a big jerk and the cause of all your suffering?! Wouldn't you think we'd need to deal with that right away? I've never seen a Dad Filter budge if there was a layer of unforgiveness underneath it. Some will refuse to lay it down – they will be angry at God no matter what. But in the end they will get to see His holiness and goodness and righteousness and His BIGNESS in contrast to their puny selves and then they will get how wrong they were to tell HIM what to do.

Search your heart. Maybe it's buried down deep. Even if you don't hear God all the time, I think He's very motivated to clear this up, so maybe you could just ask Him, "Lord, do I have any unforgiveness in my heart toward You?" And then listen and see what He says. It might be words, it might be a picture or a memory, it might be a big neon sign - but He WILL clear this up with you.

He's very motivated to get this all settled, Fred. Just let go of it and say you're sorry and watch Him come make it all better. Please?

Case Study 9 – Samson – Too soft.

Now, I'll have to confess that this isn't one that I counseled with personally. So if you'll allow me a little latitude, I'll tell you his story second hand. I want to be careful with this one because it's an example of how a Dad Filter can mess you all up, yet it's part of God's big plan. So you don't always just want to go ripping Dad Filters off of people willy-nilly if God might have put them there for a reason.

OK, a long time ago in a land far away (Judges 13), there lived this guy named Manoah. One day an angel shows up and says, "You're going to have a son, he's going to be a leader, don't ever cut his hair, let him eat unclean food or give him alcohol." Well, that's kind of unusual.

So this really special kid, Samson, is born. And he's really strong. Like really, <u>really</u> strong. So maybe his Dad is a little afraid of him or maybe Dad just wants to be gentle with him – what with the angel showing up and saying how special he was and everything. (Dad <u>did</u> express to the angel a lot of misgivings about how to raise a kid like this.)

So one day when Samson says he wants a girl from the enemy village, Dad argues with him briefly, but gives in. It seems like something that would make God mad and he shouldn't do, but Dad is kind of a pushover. So Samson learned somewhere in there that Dad will give you whatever you want or you can just wear him down until he gives in.

Misadventure ensues (Judges 14) and lots of people die because Samson gets mad. Then later on Samson is in the enemy city again at the house of a prostitute (because again, even though he's supposed to be holy and a judge of Israel, evidently Father God is a pushover and you can pretty much do whatever you want), the enemy soldiers are going to try to catch him, but he rips the gate off the city wall and carries it out of town.

He's really sure of himself, really sure God is on his side, and really sure he can do or have whatever he wants. The thing is, the Bible says that God planned it that way. Even though this stuff seems like a really bad idea, it's all part of the big plan in heaven.

So then Samson meets this hottie, Delilah, and really falls for her. But she's one of the enemy too. She gets bribed (really well) by his enemies to turn against him and find his secret so they can capture him. He lies to her a couple of times, but then the Bible says that she pesters him endlessly until he just wanted to die – so he told her.

They capture him, poke his eyes out and put him in chains doing hard labor. Eventually, he tells God he's sorry, admits that maybe he was playing a little loose with God's rules for him and asks the Lord to give him his strength back one last time. The enemies bring him out into this giant hall filled with leaders and dignitaries to mock and spit on him. He asks to be led to the two main columns that hold up the roof – and he knocks them down. The building collapses killing Samson and many thousands of the leaders of the enemy of Israel. So he killed more people in his death than in his life. He finally did something selfless and acted like the leader he was supposed to be.

Now, on the one hand, it seems like it would have been a good idea to deal with his Dad Filter sooner so that he would have more fear of the Lord, wouldn't think he could get away with so much and would have stopped whoring around. But then again, Judges 14:4 says that it was God's plan all along.

So I guess the moral of this story is to listen to God before you go trying to assault somebody's filters, lenses, stronghold or demons. They might be there for a reason and it's not for you to get them off right now. Sometimes we just have to wait and see what God does with them – and remember that He is more motivated for them to get right with Him than we are.

Case Study 10 – Isaac – Pretty good dad.

Admittedly it's a stretch to try to do psychospiritual autopsies on Bible characters, but Isaac is probably the one who had the father who was the best example of all of what Father God was like. Isaac first shows up in Genesis 21, but the stories of his dad, Abram (later Abraham) start in Genesis 11. Abraham is one of the few people in the Bible that God considered "righteous." That's a big deal!

Though Abraham waited a really long time for the kid that God had promised (he was 100 years old when Isaac was born!), he believed God. God had promised that from Isaac would a mighty nation rise up and be like the grains of sand on the seashore. But then God asked Abraham to sacrifice his son. And I don't mean like give him up for adoption or let the mom have custody – I mean like the plunge-a-knife-into-his-chest-and-bleed-him-like-a-sheep-on-an-altar kind of sacrifice him.

So Abraham took off with his son, some knives and some firewood. He got all ready to do it, was about to kill Isaac, figuring God's promises were still going to be good somehow. Then God stopped him, provided a substitute (a ram) and blessed him for his willingness.

So Isaac saw a few things from Earth Dad that helped him see Father God pretty clearly. One was that he was willing to give up His only son, the child of promise, if necessary. He also saw Earth Dad deal mercifully with Ishmael, his half-brother, even when by all rights he could have just killed him. In that he learned that Father God sends down the rain on the righteous and the unrighteous. The sun shines on the Sons and the strangers.

Isaac grew up with a real sense of the need to honor and obey the God of his father Abraham. He seems to have been pretty well adjusted in his walk with God. He seems to have had a pretty good dad.

There is one interesting thing. Both Abraham and Isaac do something strangely similar – and probably like 70 to 100 years apart. They both find themselves in a foreign land with a really hot wife – and lie and say that she is their sister so they're not killed by someone who wants her. Neither of them are told by God to do it – yet when the lie is found out, both of them walk away after the fact with a lot of wealth and blessing because of their lie! Hmmmm...

Possible Flavors of Dad Filters

Abusive –	He is out to get me. He likes my pain.
No Love –	He doesn't want to be with me. He thinks it's a mistake that he made me.
Never Satisfied –	No matter how hard I try, no matter how good I am, he won't love me.
Drunk/Addict –	Totally unpredictable behavior.
Important/Busy –	He has an important job, lots of people depend on him. Shouldn't bother him.
Suicide –	I'm not worth sticking around for. My needs don't matter. He's selfish.
Died –	He's going to love you for awhile, then disappear. I'm all alone.
Too Soft –	He's a pushover. Sugar Daddy.
Emergency Only –	Call when it's a crisis, otherwise not.
Molester –	He wants to gratify himself with me. I'm just here for his pleasure.
Hypocrite –	He's different on Sundays. The rest of the week must not matter.
Untrustworthy –	I can't pour out my heart to him when I'm hurting because he'll make fun of me and tell everybody.
Woman hater –	He can't love me because he wanted boys. Girls are bad.
Stupid –	Obviously I'm so much smarter than him. Why would I ask him for advice?
Womanizer –	Why does he love all these other people more than me? Whoever catches his eye gets the attention.

And many more flavors – and combinations of flavors.

And it's not just those, but the inverses as well! You could be a daughter to a dad that hates girls – or to a dad that dotes on girls. You could be a son born to a dad that dotes on girls.

You could be born to a dad that's not a hypocrite – he's so legalistic and hyper-righteous that you learn that God is a Pharisee. And don't forget to filter in the added complications of mixed filters from Step-Dads, Spiritual Dads and maybe even Mom Filters that are where a Dad Filter should be, but Mom had to be Dad.

One brother had this twisted mother that didn't seem to be getting anywhere when she told him to do chores, so in some kind of weird effort to get him to feel her pain, made HIM bend her over and spank HER bare bottom with a paddle when he was like eleven years old. It was all wound up with some kind of strange demonic erotic thing that was already in the house – because Dad was molesting his sisters. (And Dad was a Pastor!) So ever after he dominated women and hopped from one to another. At last count, he's been married six or eight times. All of them ending badly.

You could have a dad that is so smart you never feel worthy, or one that you can out-think and feel superior to. Too soft, too harsh, too busy, too lazy, too drunk, too many video games – you name it! Someone asked me today, "How can we raise filter-free kids?!" Well, you just try to point them to Jesus and keep reminding them of who He says He is. Help them to hear Him early in life and He'll explain it to them Himself. Connect them to The Source.

WHY DOES SATAN LOVE IT?

This lens will hold up things on so many other levels. It hampers healing. So many times I've been talking to someone and they need deliverance, they have demons messing with them, unforgiveness or bitterness they can't lay down. They need physical healing and they can't seem to get it. They've had all kinds of deliverance ministries praying for them and it never seems to work.

There are deliverance ministries out there that just go down a list and say you've got this, this and this because you filled out a questionnaire. (As if they're going to tell you the truth if they have demons. Why not just let schizophrenics and multiple personalities self-diagnose. Yeah, good idea.). Ok, you've got a spirit of lust or of infirmity or gluttony – so we rebuke them in the name of Jesus. But nothing seems to work, so they say, "Well, your faith isn't strong enough or you didn't keep the doors closed." When in reality a good deliverance ministry should sit down with them and pray,

"Lord, what do you need me to hear about this? What's going on with her that we need to deal with first? I see a fear, I see a gluttony, a self-condemnation – but what do we need to deal with first? Can we take care of those?" "No. You have to take care of the Dad Filter."

Because her Dad Filter says that Dads are unavailable, untrustworthy, will not come when you call and you're on your own. OK, well, if she needs God to show up and heal and free her, but she doesn't believe Dad's are like that, then He won't. Fundamentally, down deep somewhere she doesn't believe God will come through for her. So He won't, because if you bind it on earth it will be bound in heaven. Now, in His mercy, He may – I've seen Him heal people that didn't seem to have the faith for it, and He can break through their filters and lenses, but my experience is that we have to deal with first before we can get rid of the other things.

Dealing with the Dad Filter – it's not a demon – it's a lie, like a grain of sand in an oyster that builds up a pearl around it bigger and bigger. A little lie, like that Dad's not available and not going to come for you. Dealing with it is mainly a process of holding up a mirror and saying, "Do you see that your walk with God is prophetically mirroring your relationship with Earth Dad? That you put God in a box?"

Because over and over I'll talk with someone and they'll say, "I used to be really close with the Lord, we were walking together, I really heard Him, but for the last few years it's just been nothing and I just feel like He's distant and cold." So I say, "Tell me about Earth Dad." "Well, when I was growing up we used to spend a lot of time together and we went fishing together and we were best friends. Then he and my mom divorced when I was eleven and he took off and we didn't talk again for years."

"Huh. No kidding? Well, do you see how relationship with Earth Dad looks just like the relationship with Father God. Somewhere inside you have this expectation that we're going to be really close for awhile and then He's going to leave me and I'm going to be pretty much on my own."

Or people that have mean dads that have an expectation that I missed Sunday School, I have a lump in my breast, and it must be cancer because God is mad at me because I missed Sunday School. I didn't do the dishes, so God is going to scream at me and punish me harshly. All of that is wrong and it grieves. He doesn't like being told that He's like that jerk. Maybe he wasn't jerk but he was just busy and never had time for you or whatever. God doesn't like being told that He is like that guy.

The main way to deal with a Dad Filter is just to hold up a mirror to someone and say, "Do you see that you've done this? Do you see that you've bound it this way? That you put God in this box? That YOU have dictated the terms of this relationship and defined who He is? And maybe there's no way to avoid it because you learned it as a little kid and have no way to understand what a good Dad is. But He's waiting to swoop in and give you a hug and be Abba and push you on the swings, but you don't think He'll do that because dads aren't like that. And that's YOUR fault, not His. You can't say God is love to everybody else, but not ME because I've never had love and can't receive love. And I know the Bible says He's love, but not to ME because my badness is so bad that His goodness can't overcome it. Which makes YOU God. Which cannot possibly be true. That's just antichrist, that's just the lie from the pit. Satan tries to get you to say, "Well, He didn't mean THAT. He can love everybody but me."

Please, take it to the Lord and ask Him how you have put Him in a box shaped like Earth Dad. Because so many other things, so much other deliverance or healing that you may need can't come until you say you're sorry and ask Him to be God, to be Dad, in whatever way HE wants to. Then He will reboot you, will explain to you how to have a right relationship with a real Dad. You just have to say you're sorry and He'll take it over and He will.

The enemy of our souls, the prince of this world, loves this stuff because he knows that if he can get us to do it wrong, then God's promises will be against us instead of for us! Along with Deuteronomy 28, there are other places that talk about what will happen to you if you disobey God – individually or collectively. It looks to me like these things have already fallen on American society and on the thing we've been calling "church."

Jeremiah 6:21 – Therefore thus saith the LORD, Behold, I will lay stumblingblocks before this people, and the fathers and the sons together shall fall upon them; the neighbour and his friend shall perish.

Jeremiah 13:14 – And I will dash them one against another, even the fathers and the sons together, saith the LORD: I will not pity, nor spare, nor have mercy, but destroy them.

Ezekiel 5:10 – Therefore the fathers shall eat the sons in the midst of thee, and the sons shall eat their fathers; and I will execute judgments in thee, and the whole remnant of thee will I scatter into all the winds.

Yeah, that doesn't sound good! Have we been devouring our own children? Have we used them for our own purposes, have we cared more about ourselves than sacrificing for our own sons? What else can you call it when someone verbally, physically or sexually abuses their children? Was it self-gratification? Bad coping skills? A continuation of a cycle of abuse that started long before them? Does it matter?

That passage above from Jeremiah 13 seems really harsh. But what were they doing to make God so angry? Go read it in context. They were worshiping other gods – that they had made themselves. Things out of their own imaginations that they thought could save them. That's exactly what this whole book is about – how we make up our own gods with some of the attributes of Father God, but some missing and others added. That's what they did to make God mad enough to pour out drunkenness on them and turn them against their own flesh and blood!

How can it be said that we're not doing the same thing? We have over 41,000 denominations now in this monster called "Christianity" and we start a new one every other day.

I've heard pastors say that if people aren't tithing, then they should leave so they can get somebody in that seat that will tithe. I've seen people absolutely worn out, run ragged until they collapse, then are ejected because they are no longer useful. Judgement begins at the house of God. If we can't model real Fatherhood, how can we expect the world to know what it looks like?

The enemy of our souls has set his hand long ago to destroying fathers, destroying families, corrupting everything beautiful so that children can't grow up having a proper understanding and a right relationship with Father God. It's the lie from the pit that convinces us that God isn't there, won't come through for us, could never love us and we're pretty much on our own. "Pull yourself up by your own bootstraps. God helps those who help themselves. Go look it up in the dictionary, I ain't your 411!" All of them lies. Nothing like that is in the Bible. In fact, Father God says this;

Proverbs 3:1-6 – My son, forget not my law; but let thine heart keep my commandments: For length of days, and long life, and peace, shall they add to thee. Let not mercy and truth forsake thee: bind them about thy neck; write them upon the table of thine heart: So shalt thou find favour and good understanding in the sight of God and man. Trust in the LORD with all thine heart; and lean not unto thine own understanding. In all thy ways acknowledge him, and he shall direct thy paths.

MESSAGE TO DADS

You could be Earth Dad to someone – or maybe you're more of a spiritual father to someone – either way, you have a huge responsibility. God has made you and placed you as an ambassador of the Father. When I worked in higher education running residence halls, we had a fancy Latin phrase – "in loco parentis" – that meant that we were standing in the place of parents and had responsibilities for those young lives. Though many colleges and universities have become businesses and don't like the idea of "in loco parentis" anymore, still you have no choice. God has put it in place to reflect HIM accurately to your children.

If you are full of the Spirit of God, and if you are transparent, if you don't get in His way, then it should be fairly easy for them to make a smooth transition from you to Him. Whether they are young in years or young in the faith, their development and future relationship with Father God is going to really depend on what they learn about fathers from YOU.

You have a truly awesome responsibility. The Lord has hard-wired an advantage into the situation to help you out. Children are born really, truly wanting to believe that their Dad is Superman. They are wired from the start with this amazing love, this gleam in their eye for Dad. You have to really do some awful things to a kid to get them to hate their Dad. It's amazing to me how much that relationship can endure, how many people I've talked to who really want to have a right relationship with their Dad, even though he raped them for years or beat them or whatever other horrifying thing you can imagine. God has really stacked the deck in Dad's favor, in a lot of ways, all you have to do is not hurt them.

Of course, there's a lot more to it than that, as the Case Studies show. There are all kinds of ways to teach them things that will do them harm in their relationship with Father God. I guess the best thing you could do is make VERY sure that YOU have a pure, right and true relationship with Father God, then obey Proverbs 3:5-6.

Proverbs 3:5-6 –Trust in the LORD with all thine heart; and lean not unto thine own understanding. In all thy ways acknowledge him, and he shall direct thy paths.

Now, I know I just quoted that in the last chapter, but I'm not sure you were listening. Maybe I can simplify it for you. I know that you're starting to have withdrawals from the TV remote and you probably have to scratch something. So here's the really simple version:

"Trust God all the way, shut up, don't think, just do whatever He says."

He's the only one that knows how to be a really good Dad. You're bumping around in the dark hoping you don't break things. Now, you may have this false assurance that you know what you're doing and you've got it all under control, but that's just pride. I can assure you, ONLY Father God knows what it's going to take to raise your kids right (natural <u>or</u> spiritual kids). The best thing you could do is listen really well and get out of His way.

I learned a long time ago – they won't go where you won't lead them. That whole, "Do as I say, not as I do," thing – yeah, that never works. They're going to do as you do – and then some. You need to be right with God if you expect your kids to be right with God. You're going to have to love them when they mess up, you're going to have to show them that they're a priority for you, you're going to have to sacrifice – and you're going to have to discipline. And when you're frustrated and exasperated, you're going to have to spank the exact number of times they need to learn – and not one time extra just cause you're frustrated or angry or hurt.

Ephesians 6:1-4 – Children, obey your parents in the Lord: for this is right. Honour thy father and mother; (which is the first commandment with promise;) That it may be well with thee, and thou mayest live long on the earth. And, ye fathers, provoke not your children to wrath: but bring them up in the nurture and admonition of the Lord.

Dad, if you think there is a chance that your children (natural or spiritual) are relating to God in some stunted way because of how they've related to you, then say you're sorry and be the one to hold a mirror up to them and show them they've done it. You can be a big help in confessing the Dad Filter and helping them get rid of it. There's a good chance they're relating to God the way you do – because of your Dad Filter and what you learned from your Earth Dad. So you might want to square that up first. There's no telling how many generations back this might go!

MESSAGE TO MOMS

Oh, dear sweet moms. Please don't for a minute think that I'm demeaning your role in any of this! I know that it's possible for people to have Mom Filters, or have Dad Filters that are kind of mostly shaped by the Mom that had to be the Dad because Dad took off or whatever. I know that children are tremendously influenced by their mothers. But it doesn't translate as much to them binding God with it in the way we're talking about. They just don't seem to make the subconscious connection to Father God as easily with Mom stuff.

For the purposes of this book, we've concentrated heavily on the influences of Dad, but I can absolutely assure you that I've counseled with lots of people that were really mangled by their moms! And people that would have never survived at all without their moms. The Dad Filter tends to be a bit of a combination of the parenting they experienced from both sides. But when they pray, "Our Father, who art in heaven, hallowed by thy name," it tends to bring to their mind all that they've learned about fathers.

As a mom, you are in a good position to evaluate carefully how your own Dad Filter might be influencing your children. You are in a good position to help them to see their own filters, break them and get into a right relationship with God. If the marriage went badly, if they've been hurt by Dad, start by accepting some responsibility for it, confessing it to the kids and asking them to forgive you for bringing that man into their lives or mean things you said about him or for your part in the divorce or whatever. Then do your very best to show them who God really is and how much He wants to love them and be fully present in their lives. It will shape the kind of Dad they will be, too.

You may have to set your own pain off to the side so that your children can walk right with God. You can do that, right? I mean their souls and their fulfillment are important enough to you to do that, right? If you're not sure you can, then admit to God that you're sinning, that you have bitterness and unforgiveness in your heart and ask Him to take it so that you can do the right thing. And believe that He will. Jesus died to save you from this kind of stuff. Not just to save your soul from hell, but to save you from sin, bitterness, anger, unforgiveness and more – right now.

Please, Moms, please support the Dads. Please don't demean them and knock them down and act like they're Homer Simpson. And even if they ARE kind of like Homer, try to build them up in the eyes of their children. If not for his sake, then for the sake of their relationship with God.

In the Case Studies, we talked about Isaac. He was a good guy, but his wife Rebekah taught her son, Jacob, that you could lie to dad to get what you want, even if it means stealing from your twin brother, Esau. She taught him that it was OK to lie and coerce a birthright blessing out of Dad by whatever means necessary. (Gen. 27) She taught Jacob that Dad prefers one son over the other. She taught him to be self-interested and do whatever it takes to win.

Later on Jacob finds himself tricked by his father (in-law) and works for seven years to earn the wrong wife. Then has to work seven more years for the right wife. (Gen. 29) He ends up married to two sisters that are always in competition. Like how he grew up with his own brother. Kind of serves him right, doesn't it? But he still doesn't learn his lesson.

He still has this thing in his head that he can cheat Dad, so he works out a deal for the flocks and then tries to cheat and rig it so Dad gets short-changed. (Gen. 30) In Genesis 31, he's trying to convince his two wives to leave their home and take off with him and he lies to them! He tells them that God is responsible for the sheep being born with spots and God in on his side, but in fact, he was knowingly trying to cheat his father-in-law. Now, whether God was really with him or not, it's clear that he thought that he did it himself by his own contrivances. He even lies to his two wives about what God told him! God actually said:

Genesis 31:3 – And the LORD said unto Jacob, Return unto the land of thy fathers, and to thy kindred; and I will be with thee.

But what Jacob told the wives that the Lord said was this:

Genesis31:7-13 – And your father hath deceived me, and changed my wages ten times; but God suffered him not to hurt me. If he said thus, The speckled shall be thy wages; then all the cattle bare speckled: and if he said thus, The ringstraked shall be thy hire; then bare all the cattle ringstraked. Thus God hath taken away the cattle of your father, and given them to me. And it came to pass at the time that the cattle conceived, that I lifted up mine eyes, and saw in a dream, and, behold, the rams which leaped upon the cattle were ringstraked, speckled, and grisled. And the angel of God spake unto me in a dream, saying, Jacob: And I said, Here am I. And he said, Lift up now thine eyes, and see, all the rams which leap upon the cattle are ringstraked, speckled, and grisled: for I have seen all that Laban doeth unto thee. I am the God of Bethel, where thou anointedst the pillar, and where thou vowedst a vow unto me: now arise, get thee out from this land, and return unto the land of thy kindred.

But that's NOT what God said! God didn't tell him to cheat in chapter 30 and God didn't take credit for it or blame the father-in-law. All God said was to leave. But it convinces the wives that God is fully on their side – so his wife Rachel steals her father Laban's household gods and hides them in her camel's saddle. Then when Laban catches up with them and searches them for the valuable stolen idols, she lies to him and says she's on her period and can't get up off her saddle. Again, they won't go where you won't lead them, and Jacob taught people to lie to Dad.

This same strategy – hiding stuff in the saddlebags – comes back around against him later when Rebekah's own son, Joseph, does it to all his brothers. Funny how things keep repeating themselves in families, isn't it?

In Genesis 32, Jacob wrestles with a man all night long and won't let go until he blesses him, the same kind of coercion he's learned his whole life. Then he finds out that he wrestled with God and gets his hip knocked out of joint and walks with a limp thereafter. You would think that God finally puts him in his place and he makes up with Esau and seems to do better after that – but he kisses up, then lies to Esau and takes off the opposite direction. Then his own sons lie to Jacob because they want to steal their brother Joseph's birthright. Funny how it all comes back around, eh? Jacob obeys God and he's held up as a patriarch and hero, but his motives are always just a little selfish and colored by a sense of entitlement.

That's a really long-winded example of how a Mom can really make a big difference – for good or evil.

FAITH LIKE A TEENAGER

We have three different, identical accounts of Jesus' clear statement that you WILL NOT enter into the kingdom of God unless you receive it like a little child.

> Matt. 18:3 And said, Verily I say unto you, Except ye be converted, and become as little children, ye shall not enter into the kingdom of heaven.

> Mark 10:15 – Verily I say unto you, Whosoever shall not receive the kingdom of God as a little child, he shall not enter therein.

> Luke 18:17 – Verily I say unto you, Whosoever shall not receive the kingdom of God as a little child shall in no wise enter therein.

IF the Word of God is true and right, THEN this is a pretty darn critical point and you might want to really, really be sure that you are getting this right!

So, how are you doing on this point? Do you have faith like a child? Perhaps a parable will help.

FaithLikeAChild sits in the back of the minivan and looks out the window and goes, "Whee!" FaithLikeAChild doesn't know how the engine works or where gasoline comes from and does not worry about whether the minivan has side air bags. FaithLikeAChild just knows that Dad is driving and we're going to Grandma's house and we're stopping at McDonald's on the way! FaithLikeAChild doesn't know how to navigate the route and doesn't care. FaithLikeAChild would never even consider trying to drive – it never even occurred to FaithLikeAChild that Dad wasn't fully capable of getting the job done all by himself. FaithLikeAChild just peacefully dozes off and enjoys the ride, even if it's bumpy. Nothing to worry about, because Dad knows what He's doing. FaithLikeAChild chatters with Dad and hangs on his every word because FaithLikeAChild adores Dad. Dad is his provider, rescuer, leader and generally his real life superhero. Regardless of any physical or logical evidence to the contrary, FaithLikeAChild is just sure that his Dad can beat up your dad.

If you want to see another picture of FaithLikeAChild, try this:

> Mark 4: 37-40 – And a furious storm of wind arose, and the waves kept beating into the boat, so that it was already becoming filled. But He [Jesus] was in the stern of the boat, asleep on the cushion; and they awoke Him and said to Him, Master, do You not care that we are perishing? And He arose and rebuked the wind and said to the sea,

Hush now! Be still! And the wind ceased and there was immediately a great calm. He said to them, Why are you so timid and fearful? How is it that you have no faith?

FaithLikeAChild was the other name of that kid with a slingshot that said this to a monster named Goliath:

1 Sam. 17:26, 37, 46, 48 – Who is this uncircumcised Philistine that he should defy the armies of the living God. The Lord who delivered me from the paw of the lion and the paw of the bear will deliver me from the hand of this Philistine. This day the Lord will hand you over to me and I'll strike you down and cut off your head. Then as the Philistine moved closer to attack him, David ran quickly to the battle line to meet him.

And lots like him – Abraham, Noah, Moses, Joseph, Daniel, Gideon, Samson, Peter, Stephen and many more throughout history. FaithLikeAChild speaks boldly and fearlessly and RUNS QUICKLY to the battle line to meet the enemy. FaithLikeAChild doesn't worry about fancy armor or battle strategy, FaithLikeAChild knows that God can use anything and so he goes against the giants in the strength that he has - even a slingshot and five stones. FaithLikeAChild is supremely offensive to others because he is the most like Jesus. People think he is arrogant, foolish, senseless, suicidal, childish, shortsighted and generally impossible to deal with. As soon as Goliath saw David, he despised him (I Sam. 17:42). David's brothers burned with anger towards him (I Sam. 17:28). Saul hated him (I Sam. 18:8-11 and elsewhere). There is no end of trouble when you start accepting the Kingdom of God like a little child! And no end to the reward.

Sadly, today FaithLikeATeenager is far more common. FaithLikeATeenager doesn't want to sit in the back of the minivan, he just got his license and he wants to drive himself. FaithLikeATeenager pesters Dad to get into the passenger seat. FaithLikeATeenager doesn't want to go to McDonald's because it isn't healthy and he can't believe that Dad is unaware of the ecological and economic and human justice damage that a worldwide conglomerate like that is doing to the world. Dad is just not as well informed as FaithLikeATeenager. In fact, FaithLikeATeenager often wonders how Dad ever got along without him. FaithLikeATeenager doesn't particularly want to go to Grandma's house, but is just sure that he knows a quicker way to get there. FaithLikeATeenager doesn't doze off and enjoy the ride. FaithLikeATeenager turns the music up really loud, makes a call on his cell phone, drinks his wheat germ smoothie, drives too fast and tries hard to ignore Dad as much as possible. FaithLikeATeenager is just sure that he has all the answers and his way is best. In fact, he would really like it if Dad would just shut up and leave him alone. He is his own superhero.

FaithLikeAChild knows that he is completely safe because Father is in control. FaithLikeATeenager thinks he is indestructible because he is really smart and cool. One of them is wrong. Which one do you think Dad would rather hang out with?

Why does it seem like God is moving in greater ways in Africa and India and China? Maybe because there are more people there named FaithLikeAChild. Why do we have tens of thousands of denominations in America and endless conferences and programs and books and superstar leaders? Maybe because we are the capital of FaithLikeATeenager. In fact, we're the main producer and exporter worldwide. We're building fatter and fatter pipelines so we can pump our own special flavor of it into every country on the planet.

Are there any seminaries in America that have a "Faith Like A Child" degree? What can the purpose of a seminary be except to teach you how you are smarter and better than the people that went to that OTHER seminary – or didn't go to seminary at all. What have they really done except encouraged and taught us how to divide the Body of Christ into smaller and smaller pieces?

Who were the experts in FaithLikeATeenager in Jesus' time? The Pharisees and the Sadducees. The religious leaders are always the ones that think they're all grown up and that they know best. Go read Matthew 23 and see how Jesus felt about them. He's pretty clear about how He feels about FaithLikeATeenager. You better hope you're not one of them.

How about this?

Matthew 7:21-23 – "Not everyone who says to me, 'Lord, Lord,' will enter the kingdom of heaven, but only he who does the will of my Father who is in heaven. Many will say to me on that day, 'Lord, Lord, did we not prophesy in your name, and in your name drive out demons and perform many miracles?' Then I will tell them plainly, 'I never knew you. Away from me, you evildoers!'

If this is really true, then we might want to be listening to Dad more and obeying Him and not going our own way. Many will think that they are just fine – until they are told to their face that their new name is "FaithLikeATeenager" and that it has all been in vain.

God is raising up the true warriors. Those who will not question or doubt. Those who will go, no matter who says they are nuts. God is raising up an army of children with nothing holding them down. Children who will fearlessly wade into the battle with a slingshot (and an army of angels). They will kill the Goliaths (and the status quo) without mercy or pity. They will obey fully because the Lamb is their head. They will not argue theology or doctrine or curriculum or programs. They will just listen to the voice of God and obey. And they will bring a flame-thrower to all the structures and systems of FaithLikeATeenager. Nothing will be able to stand before them – because God is on their side.

Just in case you're sitting on the fence about this when they come, consider this:

Matthew 18:3-6 – And he said: "I tell you the truth, unless you change and become like little children, you will never enter the kingdom of heaven. Therefore, whoever humbles himself like this child is the greatest in the kingdom of heaven. "And whoever welcomes a little child like this in my name welcomes me. But if anyone causes one of these little ones who believe in me to sin, it would be better for him to have a large millstone hung around his neck and to be drowned in the depths of the sea.

Or maybe this one:

Luke 9:46-48 – An argument started among the disciples as to which of them would be the greatest. Jesus, knowing their thoughts, took a little child and had him stand beside him. Then he said to them, "Whoever welcomes this little child in my name welcomes me; and whoever welcomes me welcomes the one who sent me. For he who is least among you all —he is the greatest."

Just stop for a minute and look around and see if you or your congregation or denomination are arguing with anybody else about who is the greatest. See if you are letting God direct your paths or you are leaning on your own understanding. Proverbs 3:5-6 is pretty clear. All means ALL. None of your own understanding is acceptable. None of you directing your own paths is OK. Doing so means that you are not trusting the Lord your God with ALL your heart. And it means that your new name is FaithLikeATeenager and God is going to write it on your forehead. The first being in history to earn that name was Lucifer. If God writes that on your forehead – then, congratulations, you just got the mark of the beast.

If that's your name, even a little bit, then you might want to say you're sorry and beg the Lord to scrub it off your forehead and ask Him daily to kill anything in you that is more than about six years old – give or take.

RECONCILING IN THE LAST DAYS

I believe that now is the time for this to get settled. Not just to reconcile with Earth Dad, but to break through the filters and lenses and reconcile with Father God. In the book of Malachi we read about some prophecy intended for the last days, the days just before Jesus Christ returns. I believe that we're in those days. And I don't believe that He's going to return until our hearts are turned toward the Father. That means seeing Him for who He is, not who we think He is. That means letting Him out of the box that we have jammed Him into and accepting the fullness of who we are as adopted sons and daughters of the Most High.

Malachi 4:1-6 – For, behold, the day cometh, that shall burn as an oven; and all the proud, yea, and all that do wickedly, shall be stubble: and the day that cometh shall burn them up, saith the LORD of hosts, that it shall leave them neither root nor branch. But unto you that fear my name shall the Sun of righteousness arise with healing in his wings; and ye shall go forth, and grow up as calves of the stall. And ye shall tread down the wicked; for they shall be ashes under the soles of your feet in the day that I shall do [this], saith the LORD of hosts. Remember ye the law of Moses my servant, which I commanded unto him in Horeb for all Israel, [with] the statutes and judgments. Behold, I will send you Elijah the prophet before the coming of the great and dreadful day of the LORD: And he shall turn the heart of the fathers to the children, and the heart of the children to their fathers, lest I come and smite the earth with a curse.

The reconciling sounds pretty good, but the smiting doesn't sound like fun at all. I don't know who this Elijah might be that calls people to get right with their Dads – Earthly and Heavenly – but if we know it's THAT important (for the sake of smite avoidance and all), maybe it would be good if we helped him out before it's too late. Maybe that "Elijah" is all of us that speak forth the word of the Lord. And I'm really feeling like the word from the Lord for this hour is something like – "Stop seeing Me as you want to see Me and let me be GOD. Reconcile to Me and get things in the right perspective or else. I'm big and you're little."

And it's not so much a threat, as a statement of the obvious. If we're walking into a time when God will rescue His children from all the badness, but you don't think Dad will come through for you and rescue you – then maybe you're not His kid. Maybe you're the adopted son or daughter of some god you've made up that isn't God Almighty at all. Maybe you're worshiping a rock or a stick that can't help you. But if you will turn your heart to HIM, truly as He is, not as you think He is, then He can rescue you.

I don't think He likes smiting people. He wants that none should perish. He gave His only Son to save us all.

John 3:16 – For God so loved the world, that he gave his only begotten Son, that whosoever believeth in him should not perish, but have everlasting life.

The thing is, we have to believeth in who He REALLY is, not the shadow, the caricature, the American blue-eyed blonde fakery that we've created with our own hands. Some our other books talk about the difference between following Christ and participating in modern "Churchianity." It's not the same thing at all. Likewise, stubbornly believing in a piece of God is not really letting Him be who He is and you may risk believing in something that's not really Him at all.

If you're holding something against Earth Dad (or Mom or Stepdad or Pastor or whomever), you need to forgive and lay it down. This book is mostly about getting right with God, but you can't do that if you're full of bitterness and unforgiveness. It doesn't matter if he raped you or abandoned you or killed your mom or whatever. I'm not trying to be unsympathetic, but God's words on this are very clear.

Matthew 6:15 – But if ye forgive not men their trespasses, neither will your Father forgive your trespasses.

Mark 11:24-26 – Therefore I say unto you, What things soever ye desire, when ye pray, believe that ye receive them, and ye shall have them. And when ye stand praying, forgive, if ye have ought against any: that your Father also which is in heaven may forgive you your trespasses. But if ye do not forgive, neither will your Father which is in heaven forgive your trespasses.

Ephesians 4:32 – And be ye kind one to another, tenderhearted, forgiving one another, even as God for Christ's sake hath forgiven you.

There's no gray area there. No room to say that God will allow you to hold on to unforgiveness for certain really deep really traumatic hurts. You're pretty well going to have to lay everything down completely. Now, I understand that sometimes we've held onto something for so long that our hand is atrophied around it in, that we can't release it because it's just too deep and too hard and we don't know how to live without it. In cases like that, I just tell people, "You know you should have let go of it a long time ago, right? You know God doesn't want you holding it, right? You know it's sin to hold it and that God won't forgive you so long as you're holding it, right? Well, I know you don't know how to let go of it, but just confess that you were wrong to keep it, you want to let go, but you can't and you need Him to take it from you. Then He will peel back your fingers (break them if He has to) and take it away. Maybe right this minute, or maybe one morning you'll just wake up and it's gone. But the right thing is to confess your sins and watch Him be faithful and just to cleanse you of all unrighteousness."

1 John 1:8-10 – If we say that we have no sin, we deceive ourselves, and the truth is not in us. If we confess our

sins, he is faithful and just to forgive us our sins, and to cleanse us from all unrighteousness. If we say that we have not sinned, we make him a liar, and his word is not in us.

There's probably something in there that needs to be dealt with. Deal with it. We're running out of time and other people's lives and souls depend on YOU being right with God. They won't go where you won't lead them.

The enemy has done much to destroy marriages, destroy fathers, destroy submission to parents, to mock them as role models. For many people their Dad Filter is shaped by media. It used to be Ward Cleaver (Leave it To Beaver) or Steve Douglas (My Three Sons) or Andy Taylor (Andy Griffith Show). Now they're more likely to be shaped by Homer Simpson (The Simpsons) or Al Bundy (Married with Children) or Hank Hill (King of the Hill) or Tim Taylor (Home Improvement) and/or any of the dads from Southpark (or Dr. Evil from the Austin Powers movie "Goldmember"). If you watch, you'll see that shows and commercials are always treating dads as if they're stupid or oblivious, that they're mostly in the way and you have to sneak around behind them and it's OK to lie to them. The enemy is doing all he can to make them objects of disrespect.

I want to go back to where we started this chapter. This needs to happen. People need to reconcile with their Fathers – all their Fathers. God isn't kidding around. If He comes back and we haven't really made efforts to straighten this all out, then there's going to be trouble. And it's not that He's really mad, it's just that if we don't settle this, how can God come back and us be willing to receive Him? It's not like He <u>wants</u> to smite us, it's just like gravity. If you drop something off a high building, it will go splat. That's just the way it is. If you don't reconcile with fathers, you can't be reconciled to The Father – and that's a curse.

> Malachi 4:5-6 – Behold, I will send you Elijah the prophet before the coming of the great and dreadful day of the LORD: And he shall turn the heart of the fathers to the children, and the heart of the children to their fathers, lest I come and smite the earth with a curse.

So it really just boils down to this. How much time do you think you can afford to put it off? How much time do you think you can afford to ignore talking about it with your sons and daughters? Yeah, you might want to get on that.

Please?

PRAYER

If you are convinced, after all of this, that you have a Dad Filter we need to deal with, then let's pray now.

Oh, God. I can see now that I have put You in a box, that I have limited You in some ways and that I was wrong to do it. Oh God, please forgive my arrogance to think that I had any right to tell You who You could be to me. You're big and I'm little, and I'm so sorry. I rebuke and renounce whatever lies that I let in, whatever misunderstandings I've fed and built upon, and I ask You, Father, to crush them all. I willingly at this moment, take my Sword of the Spirit and crush that lens up into a million pieces. Let everything in the heavenlies know that we're not going to play that anymore. I'm asking You, I'm begging You, to swoop in and show me what kind of a Dad You really are. I'm asking You to teach me how to relate to You on Your terms, not my own. Please, Abba, please fix all

this. I'm sorry for whatever I let in. Please get it out and set it right. Please? In the Name of Jesus Christ, I ask You to get anything out of the way between me and You so that I can hold Your hand and we can walk right together. Whatever the enemy meant for evil, use it for good. In the Name of Jesus Christ. Amen.

As I've mentioned before, it's not enough to get the bad stuff out of your cup, we have to get the good stuff in. If you repent for the spirit of lust and the Lord scrubs it out, then you pray for gift of self-control to fill that space. Sometimes the things in us come straight from the throne of God, sometimes from one another.

I always tell everyone, before you let anybody lay hands on you and impart anything to you, always ask the Lord to shield you from anything that isn't of Him. Whether it's laying hands in person or over the phone or the internet or by reading their book, we still need to make sure that we ONLY get what God wants us to have.

So let's pray this first:

Lord God Almighty, Creator of Heaven and Earth, Dad, Abba ... please protect me. You promise that You're a good Dad and that if we ask for bread, you're not going to give us a stone, if we ask for an egg, you're not going to give us a scorpion, so please know that I'm coming to You with my heart as clean as I know how to be, begging for more of You and rejecting anything that isn't pure and holy and what

You want for me. Please don't let me receive anything that isn't of You and what You want for me. But if it's You, I'll take all I can get. Thank You, Lord. In the Name of Jesus Christ, I pray all this to the Father, Amen.

Now, if you can stand in faith on that and believe, if you have the faith to receive, then I'm going to pray this for you:

Lord God Almighty, Father, Abba, please Dad, I thank You so much for what You've done in my life and all the times that You've rubbed my head and kissed my booboos and pulled me up on Your lap and helped me through whatever has come at me. Father, there are people reading this book that are desperate, that have never once felt you or heard you or have known You love to be real. If they need it from You, please pour it out. And if there is anything that I have, please give it to them and pour out Your love abundantly on them. Please, show them how big you are, how loving and true, how available and ever-present You are. Please Lord, whatever You did for me, please do it to them, according to Your will and good pleasure. We really want to reconcile the hearts of the children to the fathers and the fathers to the children. Please be reconciled to us, O God and think kindly of us and bless us – so that we may thank You and be a blessing on Your behalf to others. Please, Abba. You alone are worthy of glory and honor and praise. Be exalted, O God, above the heavens, be magnified, O God, n us. Pour me out, Lord, on any that have a need. Whatever the cost, even if I never

get it back. Even if I never hear You again or feel Your touch. Please, Lord, I've had it for awhile now and they need it really badly. Please fill their cups so full of You that nothing else can fit. Please finish what You started in them and do not delay. Please be merciful and forgive us our trespasses and swoop in and show them who You really are. I pray all of this in expectation and gratitude, knowing that you hear my prayers and answer, in the mighty, precious, holy Name of Jesus Christ we pray all these things to the Big Throne, Amen.

Dear Children, please don't delay. The hour is late and there is no more time for nonsense. Everything that can be shaken will be shaken and you need to be ready. Let all that is of the world and the things of this world melt away. The only thing that will get you through what's coming is a right relationship, a deep, abiding, intimate relationship with Father God. It's not enough to be "saved" or "Spirit-filled" or "religious" – it's going to require intimacy with the Almighty on a scale the world has rarely seen. Men will go crazy for the sights their eyes see. But my Children will remain above it all, more than conquerors, stable in the midst of the storm, because they are planted on the Rock, on the firm foundation that cannot be moved. Rest in me, my children, and know that I am sufficient for you. No matter what comes, I will not leave you nor forsake you. Don't forsake me, don't be embarrassed of me, don't deny me and I won't deny you. I love you, my dear children. I so long for you. Rest in me and know that I Am God.

Colossians 1:12-20 – Giving thanks unto the Father, which hath made us meet to be partakers of the inheritance of the saints in light: Who hath delivered us from the power of darkness, and hath translated [us] into the kingdom of his dear Son: In whom we have redemption through his blood, [even] the forgiveness of sins: Who is the image of the invisible God, the firstborn of every creature: For by him were all things created, that are in heaven, and that are in earth, visible and invisible, whether [they be] thrones, or dominions, or principalities, or powers: all things were created by him, and for him: And he is before all things, and by him all things consist. And he is the head of the body, the church: who is the beginning, the firstborn from the dead; that in all [things] he might have the preeminence. For it pleased [the Father] that in him should all fulness dwell; And, having made peace through the blood of his cross, by him to reconcile all things unto himself; by him, [I say], whether [they be] things in earth, or things in heaven.

1 John 3:1-2 – Behold, what manner of love the Father hath bestowed upon us, that we should be called the sons of God: therefore the world knoweth us not, because it knew him not. Beloved, now are we the sons of God, and it doth not yet appear what we shall be: but we know that, when he shall appear, we shall be like him; for we shall see him as he is.

Romans 8:13-19 – For if ye live after the flesh, ye shall die: but if ye through the Spirit do mortify the deeds of the body, ye shall live. For as many as are led by the Spirit of God, they are the sons of God. For ye have not received the spirit of bondage again to fear; but ye have received the Spirit of adoption, whereby we cry, Abba, Father. The Spirit itself beareth witness with our spirit, that we are the children of God: And if children, then heirs; heirs of God, and joint-heirs with Christ; if so be that we suffer with him, that we may be also glorified together. For I reckon that the sufferings of this present time are not worthy to be compared with the glory which shall be revealed in us. For the earnest expectation of the creature waiteth for the manifestation of the sons of God.

APPENDIX A
OPEN LETTER OF APOLOGY
TO THE WORLD

Please bear with me, this is long overdue and there's lots of ground to cover. I want to make sure that I get it all out. Not just for me, but because I think you need to hear it. Maybe there are other Christians out there as well that need to make apologies and will find courage here. I appreciate your time, I know it's valuable.

Dear Members of the World,

I'm just a guy, nobody really. Son of a preacher and missionary. Years and years of Vacation Bible Schools, summer camps, youth ski trips, puppet shows, revivals, choir trips - you name it. Even went to a Christian college and got a degree in religion. I ended up in the business world, but I spent two decades tithing, sitting on committees, teaching Sunday School, going to seminars and conferences, etc. I even met my wife in the single's class at church. I'm not a bad guy, I've been mostly behaving myself and everybody seems to like me. I do some good stuff here and there.

But lately I've been trying to understand Jesus more and stuff I never noticed before has really started to bug me. I've been taking a look around and I'm having a hard time making sense of what it is we've built here. So, it just seemed like, whether anybody else says it or not, I need to take responsibility for the part I played and say what I have to say.

Here we go ...

I know you think that Christians are a big bunch of hypocrites. We say we're more "religious" and we're going to heaven and you're not, and then we drive our big shiny cars with little fishies on the trunk and cut you off in traffic as we race by the homeless guy on the corner. We average just 2% of our money to church and charity, despite that we say the Bible is the word of God and it says we're supposed to give everything. On average, we buy just as many big screen TVs and bass boats and fur coats and makeup and baseball cards and online porn as anybody else. Maybe more. You've seen leader after leader end up in jail or court or a sex scandal of one sort or another.

Well ... you're right. We're guilty of all of it. We've done it all. And, I'm really sorry.

You see our cheesy TV shows and slick guys begging for money and you get that there's something seriously sneaky and wrong here. A high-pressure call for money so they can stay on the air? Were we supposed to use Jesus as just another form of entertainment? Who do we think we're kidding? Where's Jesus in all this? Aren't we supposed to rely on him? Isn't He going to meet our needs if we're inside His will?

What happened to sacrifice and suffering and helping the poor? I'm just sick about this. I mean, the church leaders, they're not all bad guys, there are lots and lots of really hard-working well-meaning folks who love and care and are meeting real needs in the community. Some of them understand and love Jesus - but I'm just real sure those pastors don't drive Bentley's, have multi-million dollar homes and their own lear jets! I mean, what "god" are we worshipping? Money? Ego? Power?

You see our massive shiny new buildings all over the place. Heck, maybe we even kicked you out of your house so we could expand our parking lots. You can't figure out why we need four different Christian churches on four corners of the same intersection. We've got playgrounds and bowling alleys and basketball leagues. We've got Starbucks coffee in the sanctuary. We've got orchestras and giant chandeliers and fountains out front. We've got bookstores full of "jesus junk" with every imaginable style and flavor of religious knick-knack. But where's Jesus? Is this what HE wanted?

Oh, sure, there are good folks all over and not every church is such a mess, but Christians are the ones that say we're supposed to be "One Body." So even the good ones are guilty of not putting a stop to it sooner. We were supposed to keep each other in line and not tolerate factions and dissensions and greed and idolatry and all this other bad stuff. Man, we really blew it! We've got 33,000 denominations and most of them won't talk to the other ones. We lose over $5 million a day to fraud from "trusted" people inside the church! We spend 95% of all our money on our own comforts and programs and happy family fun time shows and we let 250 MILLION Christians in other countries live on the very edge of starvation. Not to mention the billion or so that have never even once heard of Jesus - or the homeless guy downtown we almost ran over when we cut you off.

We're as guilty as we can be. All of us. Nobody is exempt. We should have put a stop to it a lot sooner. But I can't apologize on behalf of anyone else. This is about me.

I know that you might have gone to church as a kid and stopped going as soon as you could. I know that you might even have been abused by somebody in the church! Maybe we got you all fired up and then just let you drift off like we didn't really care. Maybe you just don't fit our "profile." You might have piercings and purple hair or tattoos or been in jail -- and somewhere inside you just know that even if you wanted to go to church one Sunday, it would not go well. I'm sorry for that. Jesus loves you. He always hung out with the most unexpected people. He had the biggest heart for the folks everybody else tried to ignore. What have we done? We've told you to put on a sweater and some loafers or you can't go to heaven. I just want to throw up.

Look, I know you're mad. And you have a right to be. We've done you wrong for a LONG time now. There's some things about Jesus that people need to hear, but we've buried a beautiful masterpiece under hundreds of layers of soft pink latex paint. If you have a Bible handy, look up Matthew 23. (If you don't, you can look it up here - www.BibleGateway.com .) Find it? Read it carefully, the Pharisees were the "religious" people of the day, the leaders of the faith. In this chapter Jesus SEVEN times says how pitiful and wretched and cursed they are for what they're doing to the people they're supposed to be leading. He even calls them "white washed tombs of dead mens bones" and a "brood of vipers"! I don't have time here, but read it and see if we're not doing EVERY single one of those things. Jesus can't possibly be happy about what we've done to you.

Sure, we like to kid ourselves and pretend everything is OK - but it's not. We're hated. Now, please understand, Jesus was hated, too. But that was because he said hard things and sometimes people don't like hearing the Truth. And he promised we would be hated if we were like him. But that's not why we're hated at the moment. We're hated right now because we're a giant pack of lying hypocrites that say one thing and do something else altogether. If we were hated because we were like Jesus, that would be one thing, but that's not it at all. You see right through our happy music and fluffy services and you can tell there's something desperately wrong here. We're no different than anybody else - except that we say we're better than you.

It was never supposed to be like this. Jesus asked us to care for the widows and orphans, to feed the hungry, care for the sick, visit those in prison, reach the lost. He wanted us to love our enemies and pray for them. He cared about human justice and suffering, the lost and lonely. But I don't think He would have marched on a picket line - He had His mind on much bigger problems. He wanted us to focus on the eternal things, not the everyday. He never once said to go into all the world and build big buildings and divide up into factions and buy Bentleys. Just the opposite! I get that you're mad at us and I think you have a right to be, but please understand, you're mad at what we've made under our own power, you're mad at "Churchianity." That's different than Christ and what he wanted. Don't be mad at Jesus! This mess wasn't His idea!

Look, I'm really sorry. I accept responsibility for my part in having hurt you. But I'm committing to you all, dear Members of the World, that I'm not going to do it any more. Not a single penny more. I'm not going to put my faith in "Churchianity" or any leader or program or TV show -- but in Christ Jesus and His salvation. That's when I was set free and began to see that God wants and expects more of us than this. And I'm not helping anybody that's not fully committed to the same thing.

It took centuries to build this monster, so it's not like it's going to just turn around overnight. But the times are changing and we're way overdue for something new. Big bad things are happening - like the tsunami in Asia - and I think more are coming. I don't want any more time to go by without having said this. I'm sorry for all the time and money I've wasted. But Jesus saves. Really. The church itself isn't even the point. Jesus is the real deal. He lived and He died for my sins and He rose again. He is who He said He was and He cares about me - and you. He's our only hope. We need places you can go that will only teach Jesus and will not be swayed or tempted or distracted by anything else. God willing, that's coming.

Please don't think all Christians are just posers. Some of them really mean it when they say they belong to Christ. The problem is mostly in the West where we're all comfy and complacent and seem to like it that way. The Christians in China and other places are deadly serious. There's no room for anything but Jesus when you're on the run from the government. They are dying every day for their faith and doing crazy hard things because they're absolutely committed to Christ. These are martyrs. People willing to crucify little pieces of themselves every day to be more like Christ. People willing to set aside everything they want to do what Christ wants. People willing to rot in prison or take a beating or die if that's what it's going to take. People that act in pure love and never back down. I'm not worthy to tie their shoes. And there are some like that here, too, and I hope we can get a lot more people to start living that way. It's way overdue.

If you're talking to someone and they tell you they're a Christian, ask them if they're the kind of Christian that really means it all the time or the kind that just means it on Sunday. The Bible says we'll know them by their "fruits" - by the faith and purity and love in their deeds and words. When you find one that proves Christ is in them by how much they love you, ask them to tell you all about Jesus. If you know one of those fearless martyrs that speaks nothing but pure, clean, hard Truth - ask lots of questions. Truth is a lot more rare than you would think. But don't settle for soft, fluffy and comfortable anymore - that's not in the Bible.

As for me and my house, we're really sorry. From now on, we're going to serve the Lord, not "Churchianity." We're going to try to call together as many of those martyrs as we hands on them and, whaddaya know, they start praying in tongues. And they probably sound like the pastor or whoever laid hands on them. It's called the Baptism of the Holy Spirit – and lots of places do it wrong and there are lots of counterfeits, but that doesn't negate the real.

Well, if it works for tongues, what about the other stuff, like faith, miracles, word of knowledge, discernment of spirits? What about love, peace, patience, gentleness? What if those were transferrable, too?! Well, I'm telling you, they are. And other stuff that maybe you didn't even know you needed, like this good stuff that goes in the spot where the Dad Filter was. And I've seen it change people and radically improve their relationship with Father God. Not sure about this? Put you hand on your spouse tonight, or your kid, and pray, "Lord, give them every good thing I have." And see.

Case Study 7 – Leslie – Layers and layers of stuff!

As I mentioned before, not all of these Case Studies are success stories. It's not that God isn't big enough, but some things take a long time to build and they don't just get settled in a couple of hours. I suppose it's possible for an oyster to make a pearl so big that there's no room left for the oyster!

Leslie came to us with a long list of issues. She had stopped using drugs, but was still drinking. When she drank, she blacked out and typically ended up in bed with whoever was nearby. She had long ago lost count of how many hundreds of men she'd been with. She was about 40 years old when we first met her and really wanting to get right with can and start doing what Christ wanted. If I run into you someday, please give me a chance to shake your hand and apologize in person. I'm going to try harder from now on, I promise. I think there are lots of others feeling the same way, so don't be surprised if you start hearing stuff like this more often.

Thanks for your time. I hope it helps.

Doug Perry - Liberty, Missouri, USA
www.FellowshipOfTheMartyrs.com
fotm@FellowshipOfTheMartyrs.com

P.S. If you would like to help me get this apology to everybody in the world, please forward it on - but please don't make any changes. A PDF file is available on the website if you want to print it off. Audio, too. I think this needs to be said. Thanks!

APPENDIX B
OTHER KINDS OF FILTERS

There are all kinds of "pearls" we may have to deal with as well. Things that sneak up on us and we think they may even be hard-wired, but they're learned behavior. All are evidence of the greasy fingerprints of Man and Demons on our lives. All must be ejected if we're going to have the mind of Christ. They may not color your relationship with God, but they're still lies that need to be settled.

All Men Are Pigs	Warped Body Image Filter
Blondes Are Stupid	Breast/Butt/Leg/Feet focus
Mexicans Are …	We're the True Church
Blacks Are …	American Dream Filter
Polish Are …	Stiff Upper Lip Filter
Pentecostals Are …	Protestant work ethic filter
Women Pastors Are …	Japanese work ethic filter
I'm smarter than everybody	Teenagers are all hoodlums
Everybody is better than me	Old people are boring
My girlfriend is perfect	All cops beat people
My ex-girlfriend is satan	Homeless are all addicts
Republicans are the problem	PhD's make you smarter
Democrats are the problem	Have to go to "church" filter
Atheists are the problem	Fashion obsession filter

ABOUT THE AUTHOR

Doug Perry has been going 200 miles an hour with his hair on fire since November 23, 2004 when God showed him an open vision of how much God loves His children, how angry God is for how we're killing His children, and how much we have to hurry. It's safe to say that praying to see through the eyes of Jesus and be dangerous to satan wrecked his life. He had a nice home, a wife, two kids, two dogs, a foreign car with a sunroof, and a multimillion dollar, award-winning business that was named the #4 fastest growing company in Kansas City in 2005. He was even teaching Sunday School.

Then he realized what he was, what we've built, and how it looks in the light of holiness. He realized he was a friend of the world – and an enemy of God. (James 4:4) So he sold all he had and gave it to the poor – or it was stripped from him one way or another.

And it was all worth it.

Now he's the author of nine books, nearly a thousand videos, music, poetry, and founder of a homeless shelter and a food pantry that feeds 5,000+ people every month. He has cried on the sidewalk in public for days. He's been arrested on false charges. He's spent weeks at a time in prayer, fasting and weeping for the sad state of things.

And he's been spit on, lied about, abandoned, forsaken by friends, banned by pastors, ejected from sanctuaries – and looks more like Jesus all the time. He's even had people try to physically kill him! Just for speaking the hard truth nobody wants to hear. But Jesus said it would be like that. Praise God! Bring it on. If nobody is shooting at you, then you're not dangerous.

OTHER TITLES FROM FELLOWSHIP OF THE MARTYRS PUBLISHING

Rain Right NOW, Lord! - from Doug Perry
What is it going to take for God to pour His Spirit out on all flesh? Or is He waiting for us? Are spiritual gifts real and for today – and how do you get more of them?

The Apology to the World – from Doug Perry
The "Apology to the World" letter has influenced thousands and been all over the world. This book spawned from responses to that letter and collected writings about the need for change.

Left-Handed Warriors – from Linda Carriger
A suspenseful tale of the supernatural vs. the natural. What was it like for kids growing up in the book of Acts? Linda paints a picture of what it's like to be radically sold out to Christ – and still a kid.

Missionaries are Human Too – from Nancy Perry
A sweet, candid look at what it's like to be a missionary family learning to trust God in a foreign country. Written in 1976.

Dialogues With God – from Doug Perry
Some discussions between Doug and the Almighty, along with a trouble-shooting guide to help you get unclogged, get your cup full and hear God better.

DEMONS?! You're kidding, right? - from Doug Perry
A very detailed guide to spiritual warfare – how the bad guys act, what they look like, where they hide and much more. For experts only. Not for sissies. Seriously. We're not kidding.

Do It Yourself City Church Restoration – Doug Perry
What was 'church' supposed to be like all along? Are we doing it right? What's it going to take to fix it? If Jesus Christ wrote a letter to the Body of Christ in your city, could you bear to read it? What would happen if you were One Body in your town?

Who Neutered the Holy Spirit?! - **from Doug Perry** Why
do people say that the Holy Spirit stopped doing all the cool
stuff that used to happen? This details the scriptural evidence of
the work of the Spirit in the Old Testament, in the New
Testament, after Pentecost, and in the church today. Along with
help to get you unclogged so you can walk in the fullness of
what God has for you.

The Red Dragon: the horrifying truth about why the 'church' cannot seem to change – **from Doug Perry**
How bad are things? How did they get this bad? In fact, they're
SO bad, they have to be considered supernaturally bad! In fact,
it's a curse from God. A delusion sent on those that went their
own way. Weep. No really, weep! That's your only hope.

Expelling Xavier – **from Dorothy Haile**
A love story between a girl possessed by something dark and a
boy just learning who he is in Christ – and their Savior. A very
different kind of Christian novel, gritty, rough and fiercely
transparent about the realities of life under the control of the
darkness.

The Big Picture Book – **from Doug Perry**
Coming soon. Answers to some of the DEEP questions.

Fellowship Of The Martyrs Vol. 1 – **from Doug Perry**
One mega book combining:
> The Apology to the World
> The Red Dragon
> Dialogues with God
> Rain Right NOW, Lord!
> Do It Yourself City Church Restoration

A complete course; from what's wrong with the church, how to
fix YOU first, how to get your cup full and get big and strong
and then how to bring real revival and restore the manifestation
of "church" in your town as it was always meant to be.

And LOTS more titles coming soon!! And in SPANISH!

Made in the USA
Middletown, DE
21 May 2022

66018043R00076